TWICKENHAM

• The Home of England Rugby •

PHIL McGOWAN

Foreword by Stuart Lancaster

AMBERLEY

Acknowledgements

Thanks to: Mai, Jake and Alice McGowan, Dave Barton, Stuart Lancaster, Jane Baron, Michael Rowe, Lindsay Simmons, Amy Rolph, Deborah Mason, Gill and Mike Hagger, Rodney East, Richard Steele, Rosemary and Hugh Vosper, John Lucas, Phil Mead, Martin Eley, Chris Woodhead, Les Evans, Clive Hill, Graham Shortell, Barney Burnham, Brenda Lashbrook, John Howard, Brian Martin, John Mallins, Chris Whittaker, John Hardy, David Kaile, Dave Allsop, Keith Bell, Chris Bennett, Alistair Clements, Ken Bourne, Jim Gillard, Andy Bustin, Stan Hitchens, Hywel Thomas, Brain Mingham, Alan Phillips, Ruth Walker, Lynne Bohane, Lyonel Bell, Dicky Barden, Philip Newfield, Laurence Messer, Bruce Rutherford-Duff, Moira Gould, Andrew Miller, Vince Thomas, Benita Wakefield, Bob Jeavons-Fellows, Michael Moulton, John Carpenter, Tom Furby and Amberley Publishing and all of the staff and volunteers at the World Rugby Museum whose personal recollections inform many chapters of this book.

This edition published 2016

Amberley Publishing
The Hill, Stroud, Gloucestershire, GL5 4EP
www.amberley-books.com

Copyright © Phil McGowan, 2014, 2016

The right of Phil McGowan to be identified as the Author of this work has been asserted in accordance with the Copyrights, Designs and Patents Act 1988.

ISBN 978 1 4456 5536 9 (paperback)
ISBN 978 1 4456 2103 6 (ebook)

British Library Cataloguing in Publication Data.
A catalogue record for this book is available from the British Library.

Typesetting by Amberley Publishing.
Printed in the UK.

Contents

Acknowledgements		2
Foreword		4
1	Background	5
2	Pre-Twickenham	9
3	The Cabbage Patch	14
4	The Renaissance of English Rugby	17
5	The Great War	25
6	The Army and Navy	27
7	The Roaring Twenties and the Golden Age of English Rugby	31
8	The Invincibles	37
9	Harlequins at Headquarters	42
10	The Middlesex 7s	45
11	Classic Twickenham	49
12	Radio Pioneers	54
13	The Making of a Twickenham Legend	57
14	The Voice of Rugby	61
15	The Varsity Match	65
16	The Second World War	68
17	Grand Slammers	72
18	Sharp's Victory	76
19	Streakers	79
20	Royals	81
21	The Welsh Wizards	85
22	Lions	89
23	Forward Dominance	91
24	The Long Forgotten South Stand	94
25	A Stadium For All	99
26	Last Great Amateurs	105
27	The 1991 Rugby World Cup	110
28	A Professional Stadium for a Professional Game	114
29	Allez les Blues	123
30	7s Series	124
31	All Conquerors	125
32	24-Hour Twickenham	132
33	Twickenham's Centenary	139
34	A Nation Awaits	145
35	England 2015	154

Foreword

The world's iconic sports stadiums are more than just bricks and concrete, they supply permanence and tradition to the teams that they were built for.

Players, teams and supporters come and go, but the place remains.

Twickenham is our home, and it has borne witness to some of the best moments in English sporting history.

When the England team walk down that tunnel and onto the field in front of our home supporters, they do so with a sense of that history and an understanding that they have a responsibility to those who have worn the white shirt and the rose before them and those who will come after them.

When their own time as a player is over, their deeds live on as integral memories to the story of Twickenham Stadium and English rugby that Phil McGowan has captured so well.

I am sure you will enjoy *Twickenham: The Home of England Rugby*.

Stuart Lancaster, England Head Coach

1

Background

The decision by the Rugby Football Union (RFU) to build a national rugby stadium had its roots in a series of events that took place in the late nineteenth century. To understand why Twickenham Stadium was built, you must first understand a little rugby history.

Let's keep it brief. Around the turn of the nineteenth century, public schools in England appropriated a ball game that had been played on the streets and fields of Great Britain for centuries. In 1845, four schoolboys at Rugby School compiled the first-ever rules to the game they called football. Others followed and, so that they might play into adulthood, a national Football Association was founded in 1863. But not everyone was reading from the same rulebook, and a series of disputes arose. The most prominent regarded the legality of handling and carrying the ball. So, in 1871, the RFU was formed to administer a separate code in which carrying the ball was legal.

Over the next twenty years, rugby football exploded in popularity. Ireland and Wales joined Scotland and England on the international scene, and the International Rugby Football Board (IRB) came into being.

The Great Schism

Storm clouds lay on the horizon, however, and in the 1890s, a series of events took place that would have lasting effects on English rugby. The very best club players were given the honour of representing county and country. This was not a problem for gentlemen of leisure, but the popularity of rugby football meant that, increasingly, the best players derived from the larger pool of working-class talent. For these men, time was money, and they began to ask for 'broken-time payment' to compensate for the money they forfeited while absent from the workplace. The RFU refused and instead restated their opposition to what they termed 'professionalism'.

'I would rather break the whole edifice of Rugby Union than give in to professionalism,' said George Rowland Hill, then secretary of the RFU in 1895. And he meant it because breaking the whole edifice of Rugby Union is effectively what he did.

Hill's immutable adherence to amateur rugby was a stance based on principle, but it very nearly cost the RFU control of the sport. In 1895, twenty-two clubs from Lancashire, Yorkshire and Cheshire signed a joint declaration, resulting in a Northern Rugby Football Union in which broken-time payment would be permitted. Rugby League was born. The north and large swathes of the midlands, heartlands of the sport and fulcrum of the English national side, defected en masse. Contemporary observers remarked that if the RFU lost Leicestershire it would sink into irrelevance. But Leicestershire stood firm and the RFU endured. The Rugby

Union would continue, on a strictly amateur basis. George Rowland Hill had received support for his firm stance, not just from the south, but from many of the grandest clubs in the North and Scotland.

But reverberations from the 1895 split would echo for decades. The RFU maintained their hard-line stance and began handing out lifetime bans to players who participated in the alternate code. The policy was a double-edged sword, however, and the English national side, increasingly shorn of its best players, entered a prolonged period of mediocrity.

Aftermath

Between 1901 and 1907, England finished bottom of the championship table no fewer than five times. The RFU had maintained control of their game, but it seemed that ignominy and humiliation on the field would be the price of their intransigence over payment. To rectify this, in 1907, the RFU chose to invest in a facility – a new stadium and home for the national side. At once it was derided for being too expensive, poorly situated, inaccessible, not economically viable and a 'damned great white elephant'.

But this time the RFU had got it right. Against all odds, Twickenham Stadium ushered in the first golden era of English rugby. The national side claimed a share of eight of the next ten Five Nations Championships, including five clean sweeps, or Grand Slams as they would come to be known. The facility, described by some as an experiment, very quickly established itself firmly and permanently in the sporting conscience of the nation.

National sporting treasure, shrine of England, and icon of world rugby, this is the story of how Twickenham Stadium became all of these things … and, in the process, rescued English rugby.

Above: Mob football in Kingston, 1846.

Above right: The England team of 1871.

Far right: George Rowland Hill.

Below right: The Rugby School sketch.

2

Pre-Twickenham

The full implications of the 1895 schism did not become apparent until the following year, when it came time for the RFU to select a team to face Scotland.

The last time that England had been top dogs among the Home Nations was 1892. That side, led by F. H. R. Alderson, a schoolteacher from Northumberland, had contained no fewer than twelve northern, mostly working-class, players. In total, ten of Alderson's fifteen defected to the Northern Union. In one fell swoop, a successful side had been stripped of almost all its star performers. England then entered what remains to this day, the worst sequence of results in her history.

They had finished top of the championship table six times in ten years from the tournament's first season in 1883, to their victory in 1892. They would wait a full eighteen years before sitting on top of a completed championship table again. Between 1899 and 1907 they finished bottom no fewer than six times, prompting prominent sports writer and administrator Charles W. Alcock, a man not given to critical commentary, to observe that there was 'something wrong in the state of rugby football in England'. Alcock made no bones about where he thought the blame lay, openly accusing the RFU of not taking the game as seriously as their competitors. The RFU, however, were about to surprise everyone.

The 1892 England team selected to face Scotland

Name: Thomas Coop
Birthdate: 10/03/1863
Birthplace: Tottington, Lancashire
Occupation: Unknown
Position: Full-back
Notes: Defected to the Northern Union

Name: John Dyson
Birthdate: 06/09/1866
Birthplace: Skelmanthorpe, Yorkshire
Occupation: Publican
Position: Winger
Notes: Defected to the Northern Union

Name: Richard Lockwood
Birthdate: 11/11/1867
Birthplace: Crigglestone, Yorkshire
Occupation: Woolen Printer
Position: Outside-centre

Notes: Defected to the Northern Union

Name: Frederick Alderson
Birthdate: 27/06/1867
Birthplace: Hartford, Northumberland
Occupation: Schoolteacher
Position: Inside-centre
Notes: Played for Blackheath in 1895 and refereed England Ireland test in 1903

Name: Harold Varley
Birthdate: 25/11/1868
Birthplace: Cleckheaton, Yorkshire
Occupation: Collier
Position: Scrum-half
Notes: Defected to the Northern Union

Name: Arthur 'Spafty' Briggs
Birthdate: 01/07/1869
Birthplace: Otley, Yorkshire
Occupation: Iron Moulder
Position: Fly-half
Notes: Club defected to the Northern Union

Name: Frank Evershed
Birthdate: 06/09/1866
Birthplace: Winshill, Staffordshire
Occupation: Solicitor
Position: Prop
Notes: Represented Derby CCC 1889–94

Name: Thomas Kent
Birthdate: 19/06/1864
Birthplace: Nottingham, Nottinghamshire
Occupation: Builder
Position: Hooker
Notes: Club defected to the Northern Union

Name: Samuel Moses James Woods
Birthdate: 14/04/1868
Birthplace: Glenfield, New South Wales, Australia
Occupation: Unknown
Position: Forward
Post 1895: Played international test cricket for England having already represented Australia

Name: John 'Jack' Toothill
Birthdate: 15/05/1866
Birthplace: Bradford, Yorkshire
Occupation: Licensee
Position: Forward
Notes: Defected to the Northern Union

Name: William Bromet
Birthdate: 17/05/1868
Birthplace: Tadcaster, Yorkshire
Occupation: Solicitor
Position: Forward
Notes: Staunch amateur who was opposed to the Northern Union

Name: William 'Pusher' Yiend
Birthdate: 15/08/1861
Birthplace: Winchcombe, Gloucestershire
Occupation: Railway Traffic Agent
Position: Forward
Notes: Member of the first Barbarians squad

Name: Harry Bradshaw
Birthdate: 17/04/1868
Birthplace: Bramley, Yorkshire
Occupation: Licensee
Position: Forward
Notes: Defected to Northern Union

Name: William Nichol
Birthdate: 30/10/1868
Birthplace: Rastrick, Yorkshire
Occupation: Licensee
Position: Forward
Notes: Defected to Northern Union

Name: Edward 'Ned' Bullough
Birthdate: 17/12/1866
Birthplace: Wigan, Lancashire
Occupation: Unknown
Position: Forward (replacement)
Notes: Club defected to Northern Union

The 1905 Originals

During the 1905 season, a visiting New Zealand side trounced England 15-0 in front of 45,000 paying spectators at Crystal Palace. The result surprised no one, but the public interest and turn out certainly did. In the crowd that day was RFU treasurer William Cail, a Newcastle-born businessman and moderniser.

For many years, England had led a nomadic existence, playing home internationals in as many as fifteen different locations around the country. For the old guard, spectators were not to be encouraged, but as RFU treasurer, it was Cail's job to balance the books. On 15 March 1907, the RFU minutes recorded that a motion was accepted, at the behest of Cail, to finance the purchase of land in the neighbourhood of London for the development of a permanent football ground. His first business plan was drawn up on three reams of hotel note paper. The budget was around £8,000. While he set to work on a more detailed proposal, another committee member, by the name of Billy Williams, was appointed chairman of the New Ground Committee and set to work finding a suitable location.

There was no shortage of options; Rectory Field at Blackheath, and the Athletic Ground in Richmond had, between them, hosted twenty-four England matches pre-1910. Both were well served by local transport links and had already built up a reputation among rugby enthusiasts. Elsewhere in the capital there were several undeveloped sites – Stamford Bridge and Wembley, among others.

Many contentious theories have been put forward for why Billy Williams suggested Twickenham. Was it a deliberate effort to preserve the game for rural England? Did landowner Williams have a personal interest in selling off a flood plain alongside the Duke of Northumberland's River? RFU accounts suggest that the real reasons were more practical. They simply couldn't afford anywhere else.

On 9 August 1907, Cail signed a deed of conveyance for a parcel of land, described as a market garden on the outskirts of Twickenham and Whitton, for the sum of £5,572. The RFU had taken the irrevocable first step. Cail's next challenge was to finance the construction of a stadium capable of hosting international rugby.

To say that the purchase was a gamble is an understatement. There was a strong suspicion that English Rugby Union may have in fact died back in 1895. But Cail and Williams had, in effect, bet the house on their belief that the future was brighter than the past.

The truth is, it could hardly have been worse. No fixture illustrates England's prolonged stupor more so than the Anglo-Welsh encounters. Between 1899 and 1909, the aggregate score was Wales 195, England 54. In eleven seasons, the forlorn English had been unable to record a single victory. So, it was with some trepidation that they would line up against reigning champions and Triple Crown holders Wales, for the first full international at Twickenham Stadium on 15 January 1910.

List of Pre-Twickenham Venues

Venue: The Oval
Location: London
Games Played: 7
First Game: 1872 – England beat Scotland
Last Game: 1879 – England beat Ireland

Venue: Whalley Range
Location: Manchester
Games Played: 7
First Game: 1880 – England beat Scotland
Last Game: 1892 – England 7-0 Ireland
Venue: Blackheath Richardson's Field

Location: London
Games Played: 1
Result: 1881 – England beat Wales

Venue: St John's Ground
Location: Leeds
Games Played: 1
Result: 1884 – England beat Wales

Venue: Blackheath Rectory Field
Location: London
Games Played: 14
First Game: 1884 – England beat Scotland
Last Game: 1909 – England 3-9 Australia

Venue: Crown Flatt
Location: Dewsbury
Games Played: 1
Result: 1890 – Wales beat England

Venue: Richmond Athletic Ground
Location: London
Games Played: 10

First Game: 1891 – England 3-9 Scotland
Last Game: 1909 – England 8-18 Scotland

Venue: Headingly
Location: Leeds
Games Played: 1
Result: 1893 – England 0-8 Scotland

Venue: Birkenhead Park
Location: Birkenhead
Games Played: 1
Game: 1894 – England 24-3 Wales

Venue: Meanwood Road
Location: Leeds
Games Played: 1
Result: 1896 – England 4-10 Ireland

Venue: Fallowfield
Location: Manchester
Games Played: 1
Result: 1897 – England 12-3 Scotland
Venue: Kingsholm

Location: Gloucester
Games Played: 1
Result: 1900 – England 3-13 Wales

Venue: Welford Road
Location: Leicester
Games Played: 4
First Game: 1902 – England 6-3 Ireland
Last Game: 1909 – England 22-0 France*

Venue: Crystal Palace
Location: London
Games Played: 2
First Game: 1905 – England 0-15 New Zealand
Last Game: 1906 – England 3-3 South Africa

Venue: Ashton Gate
Location: Bristol
Games Played: 1
Result: 1908 – England 18-28 Wales
* England would play a further game at
Welford Road in 1923

The Men Who Made Twickenham: No. 1 – William Cail

In an age of big personalities, such as George Rowland Hill and Charles Marriot, William Cail was noticeably reticent and quiet. Born in Tyneside in 1874, he was a chemical engineer and successful businessman. He had been RFU president in the aftermath of the 1895 split and was appointed treasurer shortly afterwards.

But, if Cail was quiet, he was no shrinking violet. He was known to issue stern rebukes to any player who exceeded his expense allowance, unsurprisingly, since it was his job to balance the books. It was perhaps this responsibility that impressed on him the necessity of providing the England team, and the RFU, with a permanent home.

Cail, more than any other individual, was responsible for the delivery of a national rugby stadium. It was he who first proposed the notion to the RFU Committee, and then persuaded individual members to finance the project. It was his project management and financial acumen that then saw the archetypal Twickenham Stadium through to completion.

Twickenham Stadium is therefore his legacy, and his sound judgement is, to this day, reaffirmed by the sustaining role the stadium plays in facilitating the RFU's investment in English rugby at national, club and grassroots levels.

Above right: England at the Oval, woodcut imprint, 1872.

Right: In loving memory of poor old England, 1905.

Left: England *v.* New Zealand 1905.

The Cabbage Patch

The biggest decision that they RFU ever made was to build Twickenham Stadium and, like every subsequent decision made by the RFU, it elicited significant debate. It was described as 'inaccessible', 'pretentious', 'a damned great white elephant', and derided for being a full 13 miles from Piccadilly Circus'. Even the grass was criticised, being described as 'too long for rugby'. Presumably for these reasons, the RFU, sometime later, began to refer to the stadium as being an 'experiment' during its early years.

So what exactly had William Cail bought?

The Fairfield Estate

The 1907 deeds of conveyance describe three parcels of adjoining land, covering a total of 10¼ acres of the Fairfield Estate. Whitton Road is to the south. Oak Lane, now called Rugby Road, lies to the east. The Duke of Northumberland's River, a sixteenth-century manmade distributary, supplying water from the River Crane to the Syon Park Estate, runs west and north of the site.

The land itself is described in the deeds as a market garden and was used mainly for fruit growing, a fact that would later result in the stadium acquiring its first nickname – 'The Cabbage Patch'. The land had another use too, as a floodplain for when the Duke of Northumberland's river and the River Crane frequently burst their banks.

In 1907, Cail's experiment was a long way from completion. Two single-tier stands were to be situated along the east and west touchlines, roughly level with the north and south try lines. Each would provide seating for 3,000 spectators and comprise four, angled sections that gave the completed stand a curved, convex appearance, which was hoped would provide better viewing. The design also afforded a concrete terraced section between the stands and the touchline which, along with a concrete South Terrace and grass bank to the north, would provide for an additional 24,000 standing spectators.

Changing rooms, baths, committee and tea rooms were installed under the West Stand. A press box, facing the sun, was installed in the East. Those with a thirst were catered for by a single refreshments room.

These modifications, along with road and earthworks, added an additional £20,000 onto the total spend, without a ball having been kicked. But Cail had done his sums, and he calculated that, provided they could get attendances of upwards of 12,000 per international game, it would not be long before the RFU was back in the black. Of course, all of this depended on those people getting to the stadium.

Inadequate transport links were one problem, but an even bigger problem was public interest. England had finished bottom of the Home Nations Championship with no points in 1907, and only managed a single victory in both 1908 and 1909. Despite investing in a facility that the RFU hoped would change English rugby, so far there were little signs of a renaissance.

The Men Who Made Twickenham:
No. 2 – Billy Williams

Billy Williams might have first come to the attention of the RFU in 1905, the year of the first All Blacks tour. During the tour, New Zealand had impressed most onlookers with their all-round skills, but some had taken to questioning their integrity. By the time the side visited Surrey, rumours abounded about their persistent use of the hands during scrums, and the spoiling tactics used by their loose forwards. One man wasn't about to put up with all of this, and that man was Billy Williams, who had been appointed referee of the Surrey *v.* New Zealand tie. The game is remembered with infamy by New Zealanders, and eyewitnesses describe Williams blowing his whistle on no fewer than ninety separate occasions to penalise the All Blacks for their perceived misdemeanours.

Shortly afterwards, Williams was invited onto the RFU committee and, a couple of years later, he was appointed chairman of the New Ground Committee. He had the task of locating and arranging the purchase of a piece of land on which the new ground was to be built.

Williams, a self-made man who made a fortune in real estate was well connected with the Twickenham area. By coincidence, a family of Williams' owned an adjacent plot of land, and may even have farmed the actual site of the stadium. This has given rise to the theory that Williams purchased his own land on behalf of the RFU, but the deeds maintain that the Fairfield Estate was in fact owned by a Mr and Mrs Donald.

It was Billy Williams who proposed the Fairfield Estate to William Cail and for this he has been immortalised by the stadium's first nickname – 'Billy Williams' Cabbage Patch'.

Right: Deeds of the new ground.

The Renaissance of English Rugby

Cail had initially hoped that the new rugby stadium would be in use by the start of the 1908 season. That season came and went, as did the following year's international fixtures, but by the autumn of 1909, the stadium was ready.

Towards the end of 1908, the RFU had received a letter from local club Harlequins about the possibility of a groundshare. Although such an arrangement would have been inappropriate for an international stadium, the RFU knew that having a 'tenant' would be useful to a stadium that might otherwise only be used twice a year.

We Three Quins

As a result, Harlequins would contest the first five games at the new stadium and, on 2 October 1909, lined up against Richmond for the inaugural fixture. The Quins were an improving side whose attacking back play was built around several past and present England internationals.

Adrian Stoop was first selected for England in 1905. He received six caps before being dropped in 1907, as part of a cull that came after yet another drubbing at the hands of the Welsh. But Stoop was one of the game's deep thinkers and responded admirably to the snub.

Recognising that the English game had a lot of catching up to do, he went back to his club side, Harlequins, and began to experiment.

New Zealand and Wales had been mixing up their attacks with reverse passing and short kicking for some time. Having observed first-hand how successful the approach could be; Stoop began to develop a system that would allow Harlequins to do the same. One of the features of his new system was a clear separation of duties between the two half-backs, into the roles of scrum-half and fly-half.

John Birkett was descended from rugby royalty. His father Reginald is in the history books for having scored England's first ever try, back in 1871. He was tall and strong and, like Stoop, had been selected and discarded by England, despite having scored five tries in ten internationals. He had played as a winger and half-back, but Stoop saw Birkett as a centre, with the pace to beat a man and the strength to carry him through tackles.

Ronnie Poulton was the golden boy of English rugby. An outside-centre, possessing terrific pace and an elusive, swerving running style, he had been making waves ever since he left Rugby School for Oxford University. He debuted for England in 1909 and, in the same season, scored five tries for Oxford, helping them to their largest-ever varsity win over Cambridge.

Open for Business…

A crowd of 2,000 privileged believers turned out to see Gordon Carey kick off the first-ever game at the brand new stadium and, after only 5 minutes, John Birkett emulated his father by scoring the stadium's first try. Three more followed, including one from the captain, but Richmond's pack had the upper hand and the visitors made it a close encounter, with Harlequins eventually hanging on for a 14-10 victory.

With the stadium's first win under their belts, Harlequins returned to Twickenham the following week and defeated London Scottish 43-0. They followed that up with home wins over Bedford, Northampton and Rosslyn Park. The Twickenham tenants were fast becoming the English team to beat. Perhaps the stadium itself was lucky? Either way, the stadium was now considered fit for purpose. All the RFU had to do was find a team of whom the same could be said.

Twickenham Trials

Wales were enjoying what would come to be known as their first golden-age and a sustained period of international dominance. They had secured clean-sweeps two seasons running, and had not lost a game since 1907. England had not beaten them since 1898 and had left Cardiff the previous year without registering a single point. The selectors had little over twelve weeks in which to find a team that would not disgrace their new home.

Towards the end of November, Twickenham played host to the first trial match, between a combined universities side and a combined services side. Perhaps comfortable in their new home, Adrian Stoop and Ronnie Poulton inspired Universities to a 29-0 victory, and people started to call for the Harlequins captain to be reinstated in the national side.

The next trial match was England v. The North, held at Twickenham in mid-December. Sure enough, the selectors put their faith in the Harlequins axis and Stoop and Poulton helped England to a 30-3 victory. They followed this up four days later, with a 28-6 victory over the South in front of 6,000 fans. The record attendance pleased the RFU and the selectors went into the Christmas of 1909 believing that they might just have hit on the winning formula.

The final trial match, between England and 'the Rest', would be played at Twickenham, on the second Saturday of the New Year, a week before England and Wales would contest the stadium's first international Test match. The game was expected to rubber stamp a team that would challenge for championship honours for the first time in almost twenty years. It didn't go according to plan. Exposing all manner of holes in the English XV-elect, the Rest ran out 19-10 winners.

'Harlequin Backs Fail'

The press had a field day, and it was the Harlequins contingent that came in for the most sustained criticism. With only a week to go, the selectors were in disarray.

Their response was to make wholesale changes. Only seven players were retained, while seven were promoted from the team that had beaten them. Among these were Dai Gent, Frederick Chapman and Cherry Pillman.

Gent had learnt his rugby in Wales and had not been capped since 1906, but his ball distribution as a scrum-half in the final test had been pinpointed as key to victory.

Blackheath's Charles 'Cherry' Pillman was a flanker in the Dave Gallaher mould. His combative, attacking style had wrought mayhem among the English backs.

Fred Chapman, the Westoe winger, had impressed in the final trial and for the North. He, Pillman and Bert Solomon, an attacking Cornish back, who had impressed against the South, would be making their test debuts in the new stadium.

In all, eight players would be making their international debut at Twickenham. The press described the side as a 'panic fifteen', claiming that it would take something 'in the nature of a miracle' for them to defeat Wales. The decision to fundamentally alter the side at such short notice had been a brave gamble by selectors, but then so had the whole project.

With public pressure to remove them, the selectors kept faith in the Quins. Stoop would be captain and was selected alongside Gent, in what was perceived to be a modern half-back pairing, despite both players having been selected and discarded many years before. Poulton was selected alongside his clubmate Birkett in the hope that they might form the classic 'rapier and axe' combination among the backs.

15 January 1910

Against all the odds, 18,000 people, including the future King George V, managed to find their way 13 miles from Piccadilly Circus, to the great white elephant on a floodplain on the outskirts of London. There they would see England take on the champions Wales, who they had not beaten in twelve years. Most of those present might never have visited this part of Middlesex before, and would have looked on the surrounding fields, clearly visible from the terraces, with interest. As the two sets of players took to the field, it would have been the Welsh supporters among them who looked upon their side with the most satisfaction. Imagine their surprise then, when the home side opened the scoring in just under thirty seconds.

Stoop instigated the move by choosing to run from kick-off. With the Welsh still waiting for him to kick, he exchanged passes with Gent, before feeding the ball wide to Solomon. Solomon passed it to Birkett, who passed it to Chapman, who was in the clear. Moments later, the Durham winger was over the line and England had their first Twickenham try.

Chapman added a penalty goal before the Welsh came back with a try of their own. As half-time approached, England counter-attacked and Solomon ran 40 yards to score a try under the posts and give England a commanding half-time lead. But this was a truly great Welsh side, featuring the likes of Billy Trew, Dicky Owen and Ivor Morgan and they were not to be easily outdone. A second-half Welsh try set up some desperate English defending but in the end the home side had done enough. As the full-time whistle blew the English fans ran onto the pitch and carried their conquering heroes from the field. England had succeeded against Wales for the first time in over a decade. The Cabbage Patch had arrived with a bang!

A crowd of 20,000 turned out to see England draw their next match 0-0 with Ireland, and away wins against France and Scotland followed, giving unbeaten England their first Championship since 1892.

Success at Last

In one of many victory speeches, captain Adrian Stoop, made reference to 'the Good Fairy of Twickenham'. And he may have been right. It would be another sixteen years before any visiting Five Nations side tasted victory at Twickenham.

The following season, England won both their home games, but their inconsistency away from home allowed Wales to bounce back, and the men in red claimed their first Grand Slam. The next year, England beat Wales and Ireland at Twickenham to finish top of the table, level on points with Ireland. Both Stoop and Birkett played their last games for England during the 1912 season, neither having ever lost a game at Twickenham.

Back-to-Back Grand Slams

The following year, change was in the air. W. J. A. 'Dave' Davies replaced Stoop at fly-half. Norman Wodehouse was made captain, and wingers Cyril Lowe of Cambridge University and Vincent Coates of Bath made their debuts. Kid Lowe was only 5 foot 6 inches, but his eighteen international tries would remain an English record until his death at the age of ninety-one. Coates would play for only one season, but he made an immediate impact. Left over from the old guard were Ronnie Poulton and Cherry Pillman, both of whom were approaching the best form of their lives.

The new team clicked immediately, with Davies' clever cross-field passing setting up a 12-0 win against Wales, their first ever in the Welsh capital. This was followed up with a comfortable home victory over France and an impressive 15-4 win in Dublin, during which Coates scored his sixth try in three games. This set up a championship decider against Scotland.

The Prince of Wales and 25,000 spectators turned up at Twickenham to see if England could complete the Triple Crown. Although they couldn't quite keep up the free scoring of their first three games, No. 8 Bruno Brown forced his way over the Scots line for a single try that was enough to give them a 3-0 victory. England had claimed their first Grand Slam and had done so without conceding a single point at their home ground.

Having done it once, they immediately did it again. The 1914 season was a much tighter affair. Ronnie Poulton was the new captain, and the opening game at Twickenham is considered by many to be the stadium's first truly classic encounter.

Wales, humiliated by the home defeat of the previous season, flew out of the blocks and, after 20 minutes, opened the scoring.

England retaliated with a try by Brown, converted by Fred Chapman, who had been recalled at centre. Wales retook the lead in the second half and looked like they had done enough to win, but with just 8 minutes to go, Pillman forced home another English try. That brought England within one point, and the cool head of Chapman was called on to knock over the conversion, giving England a 10-9 victory.

England racked up eighteen tries in their next three games. Eight of these were scored by Cyril Lowe, a record that stands to this day. A record Twickenham crowd of over 40,000 people, including the newly crowned King George V, watched England defeat Ireland 17-12, with tries from Lowe, Davies, Roberts and Cherry Pillman.

Sadly, Pillman would end his England career by breaking his leg in the following game – a narrow 16-15 win at Inverleith. But England had done enough to set up a championship decider in the Stade Colombes, where they proceeded to run riot. Captain Poulton grabbed four tries and Lowe three, as England racked up a 39-13 win, securing their first ever back-to-back Grand Slams.

In five short years, Twickenham Stadium had transformed a team incapable of winning anything into the dominant force in Northern Hemisphere rugby. With only a single defeat to South Africa in 1913, England had won four Championships in five years, including two Grand Slams.

Twickenham Fixture List and Results 1909/10

Date	Game	Score	Att.
02/10/1909	Harlequins v Richmond	14-10	2,000
09/10/1909	Harlequins v London Scottish	43-0	
16/10/1909	Harlequins v Bedford	23-3	
13/11/1909	Harlequins v Northampton	27-11	4,000
20/11/1909	Harlequins v Rosslyn Park	57-0	
11/1909	Universities v Armed Forces (TRIAL)	29-0	
04/12/1909	Harlequins v Blackheath	22-3	2,000
11/12/1909	England v North (TRIAL)	30-3	4,000
15/12/1909	England v South (TRIAL)	28-3	5–6,000
30/12/1909	Harlequins v Fettesians & Lorettonians	42-0	
01/01/1910	Harlequins v Old Merchistonians	32-5	
08/01/1910	Probables v Possibles (TRIAL)	10-19	
15/01/1910	England v Wales	11-6	18,000
12/02/1910	England v Ireland	0-0	20,000
19/02/1910	Harlequins v Oxford University	5-12	
26/02/1910	Harlequins v United Services	10-6	
12/03/1910	Harlequins v Leicester Tigers	0-3	
19/03/1910	Harlequins v Marlborough Nomads	56-0	

Right: Triple Crown, 1914.

England + Wales. January. 1910.

Above: England *v.* Wales, 1914.

Right: England *v.* France, 1911.

Below: Harlequins *v.* Richmond, 1909.

Left: The Prince of Wales, England *v.* Wales, 1910.

The Great War

With Twickenham and England just getting into their stride, the world was interrupted in the most brutal and tragic of circumstances.

The clouds of war had been gathering for many years, and nine days after it was formally declared, the RFU issued a circular to all clubs advising individual members to enlist. They needn't have bothered. Since the beginning rugby has instilled values in its participants, including bravery, selflessness and loyalty. By the time the directives arrived, most of the men were already in barracks.

All that was left for the RFU to do was to cancel all club and county fixtures, 'to be carried over to the following season, all being well'. But Twickenham was not quite mothballed, instead the stadium itself was drafted into active service as a place for horses to graze, while being made ready for the front.

By the time of the armistice, the First World War had robbed nations in Britain, Europe and beyond of a generation of men. The rugby community suffered accordingly. Of the thirty men who represented England and Scotland in the 1914 Calcutta Cup match, no fewer than twelve eventually perished in the War.

Among them was Ronnie Poulton-Palmer, England's brilliant outside-centre. Regarded as one of and possibly *the* best three-quarter in the world, he had captained England to a Grand Slam in the same year that hostilities began. He was shot by a sniper in a trench to the South of Ypres, in April 1915. A warm and socially conscientious young man, he was held in great affection by his Berkshire Company, many of whom wept openly at the dawn stand-to the morning after his death.

Twickenham, 1915.

The Army and Navy

The Army v. Navy game first took place in 1878 and came to be known as the Inter-Services Championship. The fixture was held at Twickenham for the first time in 1920, but was preceded by a one-off event called the King's Cup in 1919.

The King's Cup included six sides drawn from across the British Empire: the New Zealand Army, Australian Imperial Forces, Canadian Expeditionary Forces, South African Forces, RAF, and a team called 'The Mother Country', which comprised representatives of the British Army.

Six games were played at Twickenham, including the final. After a round-robin competition, the New Zealand Army and the Mother Country came out on top with four wins and a defeat each. George V, Sir Douglas Haig and William Massey, the Prime Minister of New Zealand, were in attendance for the deciding game in which New Zealand ran out 9-3 winners.

Such was the scale of mobilisation during the First World War that, after the conflict was over, most of England's finest rugby players retained an attachment to a branch of the armed forces. For example,

Far left: Lest we forget.

Left: Lt Ronald Poulton Palmer, Royal Berkshire Regiment

future England captains Dave Davies and William Wavell Wakefield respectively captained the Royal Navy and RAF sides. Therefore, the 1920s contests were high-profile events in which players could bring their skills to the attention of the England selectors.

The annual Army v. Navy game has remained a popular fixture on the Twickenham calendar, regularly drawing over 50,000 spectators to the stadium. The armed forces are a much respected component of the rugby fraternity, with three permanent seats on the RFU council and regular pre-match appearances at international matches. The stadium also hosted 60,000 visitors during a Help for Heroes benefit concert in 2010.

1919 King's Cup Final Table

	P	W	L	F	A	Pts
Mother Country	5	4	1	81	27	8
New Zealand	5	4	1	58	17	8
Australia	5	3	2	58	23	6
South Africa	5	2	3	65	43	4
Royal Air Force	5	2	3	37	69	4
Canada	5	0	5	3	113	0

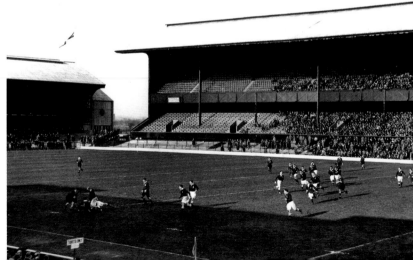

Above: Members of the Armed Forces, 2008.

Above right: Help for Heroes charity match, 2008.

Below right: Robbie Williams at the Help for Heroes charity concert, 2010.

Left: Royal Navy *v.* the Army, 1928.

Far left: William Wavell Wakefield, RAF, 1921.

Above left: Dave Davies, Royal Navy, 1921.

Royal Navy *v.* RAF, 1938.

7

The Roaring Twenties and the Golden Age of English Rugby

The First World War finally drew to its bloody conclusion in 1918. The RFU reconvened in May of 1919 and, the following year, international rugby returned to the stadium. Prior to the outbreak of war, England had been on top, securing four Championships and two Grand Slams since the stadium's opening in 1909.

It would be too much to expect England to pick up where they had left off. Of those who had represented them in 1914, they had lost Arthur Harrison, Bungy Watson, Mud Dingle, Francis Oakeley, Alf Maynard, Robert Pillman and their captain, Ronnie Poulton-Palmer, to the conflict.

The Next Great England Side

Some of their 1914 Grand Slam team did make it back, including Cyril Lowe and W. J. A. 'Dave' Davies. In addition, twenty-one players would make their international debuts in 1920, among them William Wavell Wakefield, Tom Voyce, Cecil Kershaw and Arthur Blakiston. In these men lay the core of the next great English side.

Like Cherry Pillman, Wakefield was a flanker. But, like Stoop, he was a thinker. Having watched Pillman play, he built upon his methods and set about reshaping forward play. He saw that defensive systems could be introduced to exert control over the loose and encouraged intelligent running from his back row. His chief-lieutenants were Gloucester flanker Tom Voyce and Liverpool's Arthur Blakiston, two tirelessly energetic spoilers who specialised in breaking up opponent's play and setting up platforms for attack.

It was perhaps predictable that no side would secure a Grand Slam in the season that play resumed. Scotland came closest, but England defeated them in their final game at Twickenham, earning a share of the Championship in the process.

The following season, the new team clicked and England were back at their imperious best. Dave Davies, already a two-time Grand Slam winner was made captain. The Welsh used to say that, 'when Davies plays, England win'. And they were right, he won 20 out of his 21 Home Nations internationals, with only a draw against France marring his personal dominance over European rivals. Cecil Kershaw was his scrum-half partner both for the United Services and for England and the duo went unbeaten in all fourteen games that they played together.

40,000 spectators packed into the Cabbage Patch to witness England run four tries past Wales in the opening game of the 1921 season. Only Wakefield and Mellish remained from the pack that had begun the previous campaign and leaner, faster replacements such as Ronald Cove-Smith wrought mayhem among their cumbersome Welsh opponents, helping to secure an 18-3 victory. Comfortable wins against Ireland and Scotland followed, before a closer victory away to France, as England claimed their third Grand Slam.

A rain-soaked defeat in Wales and a home draw against the rapidly improving French put paid to any hopes of a repeat in 1922. The 11-11 draw against France might well have been a defeat were it not for a late kick and chase by Davies that resulted in a try for Voyce. This was then converted and rescued England from a first championship defeat at their home stadium. But the fundamentals of the side were still strong. Harold Locke of Birkenhead Park came in to form a lethal centre partnership with Bradford's Eddie Myers. Ronald Cove-Smith was supplemented by William Luddington, who was powerful and strong and could also kick conversions. At the start of 1923, hopes were high that England could return to form.

The opening game of the season was between England and Wales and featured one of the most bizarre tries ever scored. It occurred just ten seconds after kick-off, in front of another bumper Twickenham crowd. Freak winds caused Wakefield's kick-off to blow back into the arms of Leo Price who attempted a drop-kick. The kick missed, but such was the gale that Price was able to follow up his own kick, gather the ball up and touch down for a try before the Welsh team had even time to react. It seemed that Stoop's Twickenham Fairy was up to old tricks! Wales pulled a try back before Alistair Smallwood landed an audacious dropped goal from the halfway line to give England a 7-3 win.

Three victories away from Twickenham followed, including a narrow 8-6 win against Scotland at Inverleith and a hard fought 12-3 win in Paris. Dave Davies landed a dropped goal at the death of the game against France to end his illustrious international career in style. England had secured another Grand Slam. Cyril Lowe scored the last of his eighteen tries that season. A record that would stand for sixty-six years until Rory Underwood finally surpassed it. Both Lowe and Davies had made their debuts together in a side that included Ronnie Poulton and Cherry Pillman. Both played their final game against France in 1923. Their careers had spanned either side of the First World War and included four Grand Slams.

Captain Wakefield

A season of transition was expected for England, but it turned out that the building blocks were already in place. Wakefield became captain. Myers moved from centre to fly-half in place of Davies, while debutante Arthur Young replaced Kershaw. Out on the wing, Percy Park's Carston Catcheside came in for Cyril Lowe.

Comfortable wins were secured in Cardiff and Belfast, before five tries were run past France at Twickenham in a 19-7 win. Scotland had established themselves as their nearest challengers for honours, and so the championship decider would be a home tie between the old enemies, in front of a record 43,000 spectators.

From kick-off, both sides seemed reticent in attack and created very little. Then, on the stroke of half-time, England's irrepressible captain stamped his mark on the game by driving the ball over for the opening try. After Wakefield's score, the game was never in doubt. England ran out 19-0 winners with Catcheside adding his sixth try in four games, becoming the first player to score in every round of the championship, a record that would not be equalled by another Englishman until Will Greenwood emulated the feat in 2002. An unprecedented third Grand Slam in four seasons was secured.

In the ten seasons following the opening of Twickenham Stadium, England had won the Five Nations Championship eight times, including five Grand Slams. It is a record that has never been surpassed by any side and an achievement that is all the more remarkable when considering that England had not won a single Championship in eighteen seasons prior to this period.

Inconsistency followed over the next three seasons. Scotland claimed their first Grand Slam in 1925 and inflicted England's first Home Nations defeat at the national stadium in 1926. William Wavell Wakefield played his final game in 1927. More than any other player, Wakefield exemplified the England side of the 1920s. English fans at Twickenham considered him to be the best in the world and, fifty years after his retirement, commentators were still describing him as England's greatest ever forward.

In 1928, England bounced back. Old Merchant Taylor's Ronald Cove-Smith, who had been in the side since 1921, was now captain. Young still remained from the 1924 side and Waterloo's Joe Periton, who had made his debut in 1925, was now one of the most reliable components of the English pack. Wins in rain-soaked Cardiff and Dublin were followed by a home win against France.

Echoing 1924, only Scotland stood between England and another Grand Slam. It was not a classic, but the English forwards carried the day, setting up two tries for a 6-0 victory. Twickenham had once again played host to an English Grand Slam, the fourth of the 1920s and the sixth since it had opened its gates back in 1909.

Above: England *v.* Ireland, 1927.

Below: England *v.* Scotland 1928.

Above: Twickenham West Stand.

Left: England *v.* Scotland, 1928.

Above left: England team, 1921.

Right: England *v.* France, 1928.

Above: England *v.* France, 1928.

Below: England team, 1924.

Left: Spectators at an England game, 1927.

The Invincibles

If it had been the 1905 visit of New Zealand that had first given William Cail the idea to build a national stadium then the All Blacks' return, in 1925, would be a true test of credentials, not just for the stadium, but for a national side that had swept all before it in the years leading up to the All Blacks' visit.

A record 43,000 had attended the previous year's Calcutta Cup. With the help of the new North Stand, as many or more were expected to witness a New Zealand side that had racked up thirty-one consecutive victories. The Welsh and Irish had been dispatched without the loss of a single point. Now, only England stood between New Zealand and an unbeaten tour. Twickenham was to be their final port of call on their way to becoming *The Invincibles*.

This was one of the great New Zealand sides. The Brownlie brothers, Cyril and Maurice, dominated the pack. Behind them, the unpredictable fly-half Marcus Nicholls probed defences and laid on chances for his teammates. On the wing, they had a steamroller of a player called Jack Steel, who had been running through and over opponents throughout the tour, while at full-back they had one of the game's all-time greats, in George Nepia.

George Nepia

George Nepia was close to the complete rugby player. His strength, acceleration and speed meant that he created and scored chances, but his defensive qualities were perhaps even better. He had been switched to the position of full-back before the tour began and operated as New Zealand's last line of defence. Time and again, he had succeeded in stopping opponents as they broke for the New Zealand try line. Such was his competence in this regard that by the time the All Blacks reached Twickenham, nineteen-year-old Nepia, was the only player to have been selected for and play in every single game.

But England had useful players of their own. They were back-to-back champions with home advantage, and their secret weapon was Twickenham itself, a stadium in which they hadn't lost for twelve years.

The only misgivings among their supporters in the lead-up to the game were the five changes made to their backs. Myers, at least, had been ruled out by injury, but Catcheside, Chantrill and Locke, who had proved so consistent in the 1924 championship, had not been selected. Even Tom Voyce was omitted from the starting line-up, only to be reinstated when Leo Price succumbed to injury. In addition, Blakiston, a reliable back or second-row forward, had been selected as a prop.

The Brownlie Affair

By 10.30 a.m., over 5,000 people stood queuing outside Twickenham for a 2.30 p.m. kick-off. A full hour before kick-off, 60,000 spectators were inside the ground, and the doors were locked shut as the capacity crowd anxiously awaited the teams.

From the outset, the game was contested with a ferocity that bordered on the margins of legality. Both sets of forwards tore into each other and Welsh referee, Albert Freethy, was forced to warn the respective captains as to their players' conduct. Shortly afterwards, Freethy observed Cyril Brownlie kick an English forward while on the floor. Tom Voyce and Brownlie then traded punches and, with just 8 minutes played and in the presence of the King, Brownlie was sent from the field. It was the stadium's first ever international dismissal. The English players were unsure of how to respond and an uncomfortable silence pervaded the stands.

Several minutes later, Ronald Cove-Smith put the ball down for the game's first try. But far from demoralising the tourists, the sending-off seemed to galvanise their resolve. The remaining Brownlie brother, Maurice, set up Svenson for an equalising try and, not long after, Jack Steel put them ahead.

In the second half, Brownlie dragged several English players over the try line to score again, before Parker added a fourth try for the brilliant All Blacks. With just 20 minutes remaining, England were trailing by seventeen points to three. Seemingly outclassed, the home side might well have thrown in the towel, but instead they rallied. Corbett kicked a penalty before debut fly-half Harry Kittermaster ran 40 yards for a spectacular try, much to the satisfaction of the crowd. The game finished 17-11 to New Zealand.

The following day's headlines focused on the Brownlie's sending off, igniting a debate that would rage for decades. Many of Brownlie's teammates insisted that he would not have committed the offence of which he was charged. But, many years later, Maurice Brownlie settled the issue by remarking that Albert Freethy was the best referee that he had played before, and that the sending-off during 'the Brownlie affair' had been just.

In hindsight, none of this should detract from the quality of the 1924/25 New Zealand 'Invincibles'. With fourteen men, they had defeated a fine England side and Twickenham had played host to one of the greatest touring teams ever assembled.

New Zealand Invincibles team, 1924/25.

1924/25 New Zealand Results

Opposing Team	For	Against	Date	Venue
Devonshire	11	0	13/09/1924	Rectory Ground, Devonport
Cornwall	29	0	18/09/1924	Recreation Ground, Camborne
Somersetshire	6	0	20/09/1924	Weston-Super-Mare Ground, Weston-Super-Mare
Gloucestershire	6	0	25/09/1924	Kingsholm, Gloucester
Swansea	39	3	27/09/1924	St Helen's, Swansea
Newport	13	10	02/10/1924	Athletic Ground, Newport
Leicester	27	0	04/10/1924	Welford Road, Leicester
North Midlands	40	3	08/10/1924	Villa Park, Birmingham
Cheshire	18	5	11/10/1924	Birkenhead Park, Birkenhead
Durham	43	7	15/10/1924	Roker Park, Sunderland
Yorkshire	42	4	18/10/1924	Lidget Green, Bradford
Lancashire	23	0	22/10/1924	Old Trafford, Manchester
Cumberland	41	0	25/10/1924	Brunton Park, Carlisle
Ireland	**6**	**0**	**01/11/1924**	**Lansdowne Road, Dublin**
Ulster	28	6	05/11/1924	Ravenhill, Belfast
Northumberland	27	4	08/11/1924	Gosforth
Cambridge University	5	0	12/11/1924	Grange Road, Cambridge
London Counties	31	6	15/11/1924	Twickenham, London
Oxford University	33	15	20/11/1924	Iffley Road, Oxford
Cardiff	16	8	22/11/1924	National Stadium, Cardiff
Wales	**19**	**0**	**29/11/1924**	**St Helen's, Swansea**
Llanelli	8	3	02/12/1924	Stradey Park, Llanelli
East Midlands	31	7	06/12/1924	Cricket Ground, Northampton
Warwickshire	20	0	11/12/1924	Highfield Road, Coventry
Combined Services	25	3	13/12/1924	Twickenham, London
Hampshire	22	0	17/12/1924	Fratton Park, Portsmouth
London Counties	28	3	27/12/1924	Rectory Field, London
England	**17**	**11**	**03/01/1925**	**Twickenham, London**
Selection Francais	37	8	11/01/1925	Stade Olympique, Colombes
France	**30**	**6**	**18/01/1925**	**Stade des Ponts Jumeaux, Toulouse**
Vancouver	49	0	14/01/1925	Cricket Oval, Vancouver
Victoria (Canada)	68	4	18/01/1925	Victoria Ground, Vancouver Island

COLE COURT HOTEL, TWICKENHAM

ENGLAND v. NEW ZEALANDERS

Saturday, January 3rd, 1925. Kick-off 2.30 p.m.

No.	England	REFEREE A. E. FREETHY, Esq., (Wales)	New Zealanders	No.
15	J. BROUGH (Silloth)	BACK	G. NEPIA	1
14	*R. HAMILTON-WICKES (Harlequins)	RIGHT WING THREE-QTR.	J. STEEL (1 try)	2
13	*V. G. DAVIES (Harlequins)	RIGHT CENTRE THREE-QTR.	A. E. COOKE	11
12	*L. J. CORBETT (Bristol) (1 pen gl)	LEFT CENTRE THREE-QTR.		
11	J. C. GIBBS (Harlequins)	LEFT WING THREE-QTR.	K. S. SVENSON (1 try)	6
		FIVE-EIGHTHS	N. P. McGREGOR	9
		FIVE-EIGHTHS	M. NICHOLLS (1 pen goal) (1 gl)	12
10	H. J. KITTERMASTER (Oxford) (1 try)	STAND-OFF HALF		
9	*A. T. YOUNG (Cambridge)	SCRUM HALF	J. C. MILL	14
		WING FORWARD	J. H. PARKER (1 try)	15
1	*W. W. WAKEFIELD (Harlequins)	FORWARD	Q. DONALD	20
2	*R. COVE-SMITH (Old Merchant Taylors) (1 try)	FORWARD	W. R. IRVINE	18
3	*A. T. VOYCE (Gloucester)	FORWARD	M. J. BROWNLIE (1 try)	21
4	*A. F. BLAKISTON (Liverpool)	FORWARD	R. R. MASTERS	26
5	*G. S. CONWAY (Rugby) (Gl)	FORWARD	C. J. BROWNLIE ordered off (kicking)	27
6	*J. S. TUCKER (Bristol)	FORWARD	A. WHITE	22
7	R. J. HILLARD (Oxford)	FORWARD	J. RICHARDSON	23
8	*R. EDWARDS (Newport)	FORWARD		

*Internationals.

NZ won

NZ 1 gl 1 pen gl 3 tries = 17 pts
England 1 gl 1 pen gl 1 try = 11 pts

Above: New Zealand try, 1925.

Above right: George Conway, Tom Voyce and William Wavell Wakefield.

Below right: Prince of Wales.

Left: England *v.* New Zealand programme, 1925.

9

Harlequins at Headquarters

'Talk about Twickenham being the cradle of Rugby Union. If they hadn't agreed to us playing there it would have been a damned great white elephant.'

(Unnamed) Harlequin Official

It was Adrian Stoop himself who had first proposed a groundshare. Harlequins were a venerable old club, formed out of the ashes of Hampstead FC in 1869 and founder members of the Rugby Football Union. Since then they had led a nomadic existence, playing in several North London locations before latterly moving west across the city. Stoop knew, however, that if his side were to prosper it would need a permanent home.

It would have been inappropriate for the national association to groundshare with a club side but there were obvious benefits in having a tenant. Without one the stadium might only be used twice a season for international fixtures. A two-year tenancy was agreed before Stoop requested that it be extended to five. The RFU agreed to the proposal on the condition that all of Harlequins home first-team fixtures be played at the stadium.

The arrangement suited Harlequins well. Between 1909 and 1990, they played 760 games at Twickenham, winning 448 of them. There were considerable benefits for their players in playing in the shop window as it were. Dai Gent, who played in the first international match at the stadium, had made reference to Harlequin favouritism even before a ball had been kicked. Adrian Stoop, William Wavell Wakefield, Bob Hiller, Will Carling and Chris Robshaw are just a few Harlequin players who have gone on to captain their country.

At the end of the Second World War, the RFU restricted the side's usage of the stadium to fourteen games per season and, in 1963, Harlequins built their own stadium, appropriately named, the Stoop. In 1990, Harlequins played the final game of a Twickenham tenancy that had spanned ten decades.

Since 2008, the tradition has been rekindled, with Harlequins playing a number of home fixtures in front of sell-out crowds as part of the London Double Header and annual Big Game fixture in between Christmas and New Year.

Interestingly, Harlequins' ground tenancy agreement has never formally ended...

Right: Harlequins v. Coventry, 1960.

Above: Nim Hall, Harlequins, 1951.

Below: Harlequins dressing room sign.

Nomadic Quins

1867–69	Hampstead
1869/70	Finchley Road
1870/71	Highbury Vale
1871/72	Tufnell Park
1872/73	Belsize Road
1873/74	Putney Heath
1874/75	Kensal Green
1875/76	Stamford Brook
1876–78	Turnham Green
1878–83	Devonshire Park
1883–97	Chiswick Park
1897–99	Catford
1899/00	Wimbledon Park
1907–09	Wandsworth Common
1909–90	Twickenham
1925–63	Teddington
1963–present	Twickenham Stoop

HARLEQUINS

10

The Middlesex 7s

For many years, the least developed side of Twickenham Stadium was the south. At the end of the First World War, the exposed concrete terrace was extended and a clock tower constructed at the back. The clock tower didn't last long, but the terrace remained for over sixty years and, from 1926 onwards, was the site of English rugby's biggest annual end-of-season party.

The Middlesex 7s began life as a southern counterpart to the popular Melrose 7s that had taken place in the Scottish Borders since the seven-man game had been invented there by a butcher, Ned Haig, in 1883.

Appropriately a London-based Scot called Dr Russell-Cargill instigated the tournament which quickly became something of an end-of-season bash, featuring between twelve and sixteen sides.

Harlequins dominated the early years, winning the first four tournaments. Ever-present in the competition, they eventually bettered the winning streak sixty years later by winning five consecutive tournaments between 1986 and 1990.

The list of winners is dominated by London sides, with a few notable exceptions. The Barbarians won in 1934, 1997 and 1998, Western Samoa in 1992 and there were also two successful incursions by Rugby League sides: Wigan Warriors winning in 1996, and Bradford Bulls in 2002.

The tournament peaked in popularity in the 1980s, attracting upwards of 60,000 spectators, but an increase in competitive rugby lead to several format alterations during the professional age. The competition was held at Twickenham for the final time in 2011.

Twickenham may have seen the last of this classic tournament, but a keg of ale opened and shared around the South Terrace at the Middlesex 7s represent the very best of times at Twickenham for rugby fans of a certain age.

South Terrace, 1931.

List of Winners

1926	Harlequins	1955	Richmond	1984	London Welsh
1927	Harlequins	1956	London Welsh	1985	London Wasps
1928	Harlequins	1957	St Luke's College	1986	Harlequins
1929	Harlequins	1958	Blackheath	1987	Harlequins
1930	London Welsh	1959	Loughborough Colleges	1988	Harlequins
1931	London Welsh	1960	London Scottish	1989	Harlequins
1932	Blackheath	1961	London Scottish	1990	Harlequins
1933	Harlequins	1962	London Scottish	1991	London Scottish
1934	Barbarians	1963	London Scottish	1992	Western Samoa
1935	Harlequins	1964	Loughborough Colleges	1993	London Wasps
1936	Sale	1965	London Scottish	1994	Bath
1937	London Scottish F. C.	1966	Loughborough Colleges	1995	Leicester Tigers
1938	Metropolitan Police	1967	Harlequins	1996	Wigan Warriors (RL)
1939	Cardiff	1968	London Welsh	1997	Barbarians
1940	St Mary's Hospital	1969	St Luke's College, Exeter	1998	Barbarians
1941	Cambridge University R. U. F. C.	1970	Loughborough Colleges	1999	Penguins
1942	St Mary's Hospital	1971	London Welsh	2000	Penguins
1943	St Mary's Hospital	1972	London Welsh	2001	British Army
1944	St Mary's Hospital	1973	London Welsh	2002	Bradford Bulls (RL)
1945	Nottingham	1974	Richmond	2003	Northampton Saints
1946	St Mary's Hospital	1975	Richmond	2004	British Army
1947	Rosslyn Park	1976	Loughborough Colleges	2005	Gloucester
1948	London Wasps	1977	Richmond	2006	London Wasps
1949	Heriot's FP	1978	Harlequins	2007	Newcastle Falcons
1950	Rosslyn Park	1979	Richmond	2008	Harlequins
1951	Richmond	1980	Richmond	2009	London Irish
1952	London Wasps	1981	Rosslyn Park	2010	ULR Samurai
1953	Richmond	1982	Stewart's Melville Former Pupils	2011	Samurai International
1954	Rosslyn Park	1983	Richmond		

Above: Harlequins Middlesex 7s, 1933.

Above right: Harlequins and Rosslyn Park play sackball, Middlesex 7s, 1929.

Below right: Harlequins *v.* Wasps, Middlesex 7s, 1952.

Above: Rosslyn Park, Middlesex 7s, 1981.

Left: Middlesex 7s poster, 1935.

11

Classic Twickenham

William Cail had been pleased to record a £2,000 return on the RFU's investment, after England's first test match at Twickenham back in 1910. Around 18,000 spectators had attended that inaugural fixture against Wales. Since then, minor ground alterations and the improved fortunes of the England side had seen crowds swell to 30,000 in 1914, and 43,000 by 1924.

Cail was still around in 1924, and his last act as Honorary Treasurer was to instruct the respected architect, Archibald Leitch, to plan the construction of a North Stand. Leitch had acquired his reputation by designing and building two-storey stands at Ibrox, Roker and Villa Park, among others. His new North Stand would provide 3,515 new seats and space for 7,118 standing spectators.

The stand was opened in 1924, just in time for the visit of New Zealand and the RFU was rewarded with a record 60,000 gate. But in spite of these improvements it had not gone unnoticed by Cail's successors that thousands more had been locked outside of the stadium, which had been declared full over an hour before kick-off. It was clear that the stadium remained ripe for expansion.

'Twickers'

Prior to the construction of the North Stand, a Motor Park directly west of the stadium had been cleared and levelled. The 1920s had seen an explosion in the use of motor cars in and around London. Mass production techniques had made cars cheaper, but private cars remained a luxury that only the well-to-do could afford. This wasn't a problem for the Twickenham set, however, who seemed actually to enjoy queuing along Whitton Road on their way to the big game. A new generation of rugby enthusiast began to refer to Twickenham affectionately as 'Twickers' and champagne picnics out of food hampers, balanced in the boot of the car while parked in the West Car Park, became a pre-match ritual that has endured to this day.

In 1927, the RFU approved the extension of the East Stand. The proposal was not to replace the existing stand but to construct a second tier over the existing structure, effectively doubling its size. Work was completed before the end of 1927, and the RFU were rewarded with a record crowd of 70,000 against France during the 1928 season. With those numbers, the stadium would quickly pay for itself, but now Twickenham, not for the last time, had a peculiarly lop-sided feel to it.

The construction of the North Stand and extension of the East confirmed that the stadium was here to stay. But in the winter of 1928, nature chose to remind everyone of one of the biggest misgivings about the location of the stadium in the first place.

Christmas of 1927 had seen heavy snowfall around the south of England and the source of the Thames. The ice persisted until two days before England were due to face Australia/New South Wales in January of 1928, when the onset of heavy rain caused the snow to melt. Inevitably, the Thames and several of its tributaries, including the Crane and Duke of Northumberland's River, burst their banks. A wave of water spread across the old floodplain, now the West Car Park, as far as Whitton Road.

On the corner of Whitton Road and Oak Lane stood Rugby Lodge, a large old house where RFU assistant secretary Hubert Langley lived with his family. Hubert's daughter recalled water flooding the ground floor of the property up to waist height, inflicting damage that would later necessitate the demolition of the house. Other observers noted that a boat could have been sailed around the back of the South Terrace. Needless to say, the game against the Australians went ahead as planned.

Rugby's Amateur Heyday

Also in 1928, that old RFU stalwart, George Rowland-Hill, passed away. Hill's staunch defence of amateur rugby had very nearly cost the RFU its custodianship of the English game back in 1895, but in Twickenham Stadium he had lived to see it reborn in an image which he approved. To reiterate the RFU's commitment to Hill's actions, RFU secretary Charles Marriot arranged a permanent memorial to his predecessor in the shape of the Rowland Hill Memorial Gates, which were formally unveiled before an invitation England & Wales v. Scotland & Ireland game in 1929.

The 1929 season opened with another English home victory over the Welsh. The game was a very visible reminder that, despite recent expansion, the stadium was still not fully meeting demand. Several hundred Welsh supporters had failed to get tickets before the ground sold out, and a dozen of the more tenacious men and boys among them caught sight of their heroes by spending the best part of two hours up a large tree, just outside one of the main access gates.

With the conversion of the East Stand having worked so satisfactorily, work began on a similar process in the West in 1930. Unlike the East, the West would require a number of special innovations. As well as the home and away dressing rooms, spacious enough to contain eight giant baths, a president's room, large committee room, royal retiring room as well as several new tearooms and bars, would be housed under the stand. The majority of this would be hidden behind a delicate brick façade, with a sign saying 'Office', that would be the public face of the RFU for the next sixty years.

The South Terrace was extended once again and by 1932 the five-year period of stadium expansion was at an end. The stadium was now able to accommodate upwards of 70,000 spectators in comfort, and attendances for international games didn't fall below 60,000 for the remainder of the decade, peaking at 73,000 in the game against New Zealand in 1936.

Twickenham had now entered its 'heyday' period with a stadium architecture that would comprise the 'Twickenham Look' right up until the 1980s.

Above: Kneller Road flood.

Above right: East Stand, 1927.

Below right: Chertsey Road opens, 1933.

Left: Spectators risk life and limb to catch the England *v.* Wales game, 1929.

Above: North Stand, 1924.

Above right: Photograph used on the front of the match-day programme, showing the North, East and West Stands complete, 1932.

Above far right: West Stand offices, 1959.

Below far right: Rowland Hill Memorial gates unveiling, 1929.

Below right: West car park, 1932.

12

Radio Pioneers

The year 1927 witnessed a curious new addition to the rear of the South Terrace. A little known company called the British Broadcasting Corporation was granted permission to construct what looked like a bird's nest on top of the fence at the back. The strange wooden cube, accessed via a short ladder, was greeted with utter bemusement by fans prior to the 1927 England *v.* Wales match. Little did they know that they were witnessing history in the making. Twickenham was about to play host to the first ever live radio team sports commentary broadcast.

England won the game by eleven points to nine. If any of those clustered on the South Terrace had taken a break from the game and turned around they might have seen a strange man, wearing a large pair of headphones, leaning casually against the wooden box. Inside, behind the microphone, was former Harlequin Teddy Wakelam.

Wakelam had been given one firm instruction by his employers before the broadcast began. The words 'don't swear' were pinned at eye level on the inside of the wooden commentary box. The following week he would deliver the first live football commentary and he covered test cricket and Wimbledon later the same year. In those early years, Wakelam was *the* voice of British sports broadcasting, but he would go on to become synonymous with rugby, a game that he loved. He went on broadcasting right up to and beyond the Second World War.

Before 1939, Wakelam pioneered a technique called 'grid commentary'. It relied on *The Radio Times* to provide a reference card that divided the Twickenham pitch into a grid. The listener would place the card in front of the wireless while listening to the game. While the game was in play, Wakelam would refer to the position of the ball by its position on the grid. The technique, abandoned after the Second World War, was the norm up until 1939, adding the phrase 'back to square one' to the national lexicon.

Right: South-east corner, 1967.

Above: The Radio Times.

Above left: Teddy Wakelam, 1927.

Below left: Radio commentary box, 1927.

13

The Making of a Twickenham Legend

England began the 1930s with another championship win, despite losing to Ireland and drawing at home with Scotland. Grand Slams were off the agenda from 1931 onwards, as the French were excluded from the tournament on the grounds of professionalism and it reverted back to the Home Nations Championship.

The 1930s could never quite live up to the highs of the 1920s, but they did include two very good teams and a handful of exceptional players. Scrum-half Bernard Gadney had made an impression on selectors with his athleticism and physicality, and made his test debut in 1932. Two years later, he became the first Leicester Tigers player to captain England.

The same year brought a further two solid additions to the side in the shape of unpredictable, South African-born, full-back Tuppy Owen-Smith and centre Peter Cranmer. Owen-Smith was a strong attacking full-back. He was also a champion lightweight boxer and had played cricket for South Africa. Cranmer was a more orthodox running centre and also a first-class cricketer.

In 1934, a front-row led by Northampton's Ray Longland earned England victories in Cardiff and Dublin to set up a Championship decider against Scotland at Twickenham. In the event, as is so often the case between these two sides, the game was a trial of attrition, but England did enough to edge the Scots 6-3, and England had picked up their first Triple Crown and championship clean sweep since 1928.

Inconsistency marred the 1935 season, but the following year a brace of exciting wingers were made ready for the season-opener at Twickenham and the long-awaited return of the All Blacks. Sale's Hal Sever would gain a solid reputation as the scorer of crucial tries over several seasons, but his try-scoring debut was overshadowed by the gentleman on the other wing, with whom the 1936 England New Zealand test will be forever associated.

Obo

Prince Alexander Obolensky was born into the Russian nobility, on the eve of the 1917 Bolshevik takeover. His family had fled and the young prince had grown up in Muswell Hill, North London. He had first played rugby at Trent College and became a blue for Oxford University in 1935. It was around about this time that he came to the attention of the England selectors. Obolensky was good, but there was a major snag – he was Russian. A British passport was secured, sparking a significant public debate about the nature of citizenship. Even the Prince of Wales is purported to have questioned his fellow blue blood on the matter prior to kick-off.

A crowd of 73,000 assembled to watch the final test-match of New Zealand's 1935/36 tour. Though not quite 'The Invincibles', the side was typically strong and captained by a giant of a flanker called Jack 'Luggy' Manchester. England had never beaten New Zealand, but hopes were high that Gadney's team were on the verge of history.

Obo, possessing lighting speed, had even fashioned his own light weight boots to further aid his running. Close to the twenty minute mark, he tore around the outside of the Kiwi full-back and ran a try in from forty yards out. Twickenham was on its feet. Panicked by Obolensky's pace, the All Blacks sent men over to the left flank to cover his runs. When Candler found him again he adjusted his body and zipped diagonally towards the left-hand corner of the try line, evading the outstretched hands of two wrong-footed defenders. Once more the crowd erupted. The debate over Obolensky's nationality was emphatically settled.

Hal Sever added a 35-yard try of his own in the second half and England had sealed a famous 13-0 victory. The presence of two Pathé News cameras meant that rugby fans all over the British Empire could enjoy watching the victory. The myth of the 'Invincible' all-conquering All Black had been laid truly to rest at Twickenham.

Years later, Bernard Gadney would comment that the English pack had been the deciding factor in their victory, as evidenced by the fact that Owen-Smith hadn't needed to make a single defensive interception in the whole game, but by then the émigré Prince and the Obolensky Game had already become an established part of Twickenham and English sporting folklore.

Most of the side was still intact in 1937 when England claimed another Championship win and Triple Crown. Fly-half Tommy Kemp was brought into the side and Owen-Smith was made captain, as Hal Sever put in two match-winning performances at Twickenham, drop-kicking England to a 4-3 win over Wales, and scoring a barnstorming try in the dying stages of the England Ireland match to give the home side a 9-8 victory.

Prince Alexander Obolensky gained all four of his international caps in the 1936 season. In 1938, he joined the Royal Air Force Volunteer Reserve, and in 1940 the Prince was tragically killed in a training exercise. He was aged just twenty-three.

Above: Scotland supporters, 1932.

Above right: England *v.* New Zealand, 1936.

Below right: London Transport poster, 1936.

Left: England *v.* Ireland, 1937.

All-Blacks at TWICKENHAM

v London Counties BOXING DAY at 2.15

England *v.* Scotland, 1934.

14

The Voice of Rugby

In 1938, an innovation that would have a profound bearing on the game of rugby, was trialled at Twickenham Stadium. The 52nd Calcutta Cup would be played out in front of cameras that would broadcast the game *live* on television.

Film recordings were not new, Pathé News had been making recordings since the 1920s. At full-time they would can their film reels and transport them, by motorcycle, into town for editing and duplication. They would be shown in cinemas around the country the following week.

Anyone who actually owned a television in 1938 was in for a rare treat. England went into the game knowing that a win would allow them to retain a share of the championship with Wales and Scotland. Scotland, however, knew that a win would give them the championship, Triple Crown and Calcutta Cup.

Six tries were registered in a game in which the impetus swung from one side to the other multiple times. With seconds left, and Scotland defending a slender lead, Robert Wilson Shaw scored one of the stadium's finest tries by running diagonally across the north-west corner of the try line, sparking a Scottish pitch invasion and securing the spoils for the visiting side. Scotland had won the first ever live broadcast rugby match, but few of the English fans left the stadium disappointed at having witnessed so fine a contest.

The year 1938, however, turned out to be little more than a prelude, with the events of the Second World War taking international rugby off the agenda for many years. But, in 1952, a representative of the BBC met with representatives of the four home unions to discuss further broadcasts. The unions unanimously agreed to reject the proposal, for fear that live broadcasting would damage club attendances. The following year the RFU canvassed the opinions of its members, fully expecting them to support their stance in the matter. To their surprise, their members overwhelmingly supported the BBC proposal. The RFU adjusted their position accordingly, but it would be a further two years before the four unions could come to an agreement that facilitated live broadcasts.

Once this was agreed, a large wooden box with a glass window, known as a 'boat', was bolted onto the front of the section of the West Stand that separated the upper and lower tiers, giving commentators a bird's eye view of the game.

The Voice of Rugby

Over time commentator's voices have become even more recognisable than the players. Welshman and former Lions' captain Cliff Morgan was probably the first commentator to be taken to heart for his vocal craft, delivering the following memorable lines while watching the Barbarians score against New Zealand in 1973: 'If the greatest writer of the written word would've written that story no one would have believed it.'

That same decade, rugby became forever entwined with the lilting affection of a PE teacher from the Scottish borders. Bill McLaren started out on the radio but progressed to television as the new medium grew in popularity. His preparation before matches was meticulous. For each game he produced extensive colour-coded notes, detailing every interesting statistic and vignette about both teams, and all of the players. Throughout the 1970s, 1980s and 1990s, he dominated live television rugby broadcasting and had come to be regarded as the 'Voice of Rugby' by the time he retired in 2000.

By this time, television had worked its most profound impact on the culture of the game. The first two World Cups had exposed rugby to unprecedented levels of media exposure and, in 1995, national unions found out to their alarm that they were in imminent danger of losing control of their sport.

Rupert Murdoch's BSkyB, with the intention of setting up rival professional leagues and governing bodies, had approached and secured the support of many of rugby's greatest stars. The International Rugby Board called a special meeting in August and, in many cases reluctantly, agreed the repeal of amateur regulations. Almost 100 years to the day since George Rowland Hill threatened to 'break the whole edifice' of Rugby Union, the sport had reneged on his commitments. After 1995, Rugby Union would operate on a professional basis.

This meant more television coverage than ever by national and subscription broadcasters and latterly online. Rugby commentary and analysis has become a professional vocation in its own right, with many of Twickenham's former gladiators taking their turn behind the microphone.

In 2000, the Office of Communications (Ofcom) declared that the Six Nations was to be a Category B 'protected sporting event', meaning that the BBC's stable of reporters and commentators would continue to broadcast the tournament 'free-to-air'. Eddie Butler's rambling poetic musings, as well as his entertaining debates with agreeable sidekick Brian Moore, have remained a staple part of British test-rugby ever since.

Above: Cameraman gantry, 2011.

Right: Broadcaster, 2009.

Above: England *v.* Wales, 1970.

Left: Bill McLaren's notes, England *v.* Scotland, 1991.

15

The Varsity Match

The Varsity Match was first contested in 1872, a year after the first international match. It was moved permanently to Twickenham in 1921 and has remained an annual fixture ever since. Traditionally held on a Tuesday, it has more recently been moved to a Thursday, in the winter month of December.

The 100th game, staged in 1981, is one of the few games to have been played on snow, owing to overnight snowfall that groundstaff were unable to shift.

The game regularly attracts upwards of 30,000 spectators and has always been of a very high standard. Ronnie Poulton, Mike Gibson, Gerald Davies, David Kirk, Rob Andrew and Gavin Hastings are just a few to have taken part in the game over the years.

Right: Varsity Match, 1924.

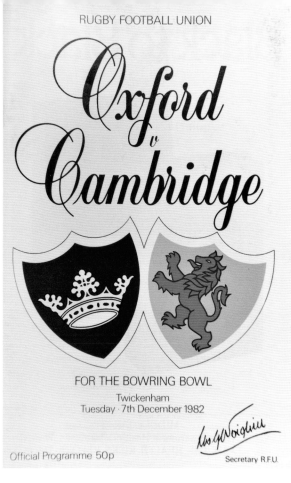

Above: Match programme, 1982.

Right: Varsity fans, 2011.

Left: William Wavell Wakefield and King George V, Varsity Match, 1922.

16

The Second World War

The Second World War broke out on 1 September 1939 and, as in 1914, the RFU cancelled their fixtures so that the nation might focus their attentions on the war effort. Two full-time members of staff were retained by the RFU to watch over the stadium during the course of the Second World War – RFU secretary Sydney Coopper and groundsman Charlie Hale. But despite the prolonged break in play, the stadium would not remain idle. Instead it was requisitioned and put into active service as a civil defence depot.

Twickenham Civil Defence Depot

The West car park, which had built up a reputation during the inter-war years as a respectable venue for champagne picnics, now found itself transformed into a coal dump. Its southern extremity and the space underneath the South Terrace were taken over by the National Fire Service, as a depositary for the vehicles, pumps and appliances that would see action during the Blitz years of 1940 and 1941.

The East car park was dug up and temporarily turned back into a cabbage patch, and an air-raid shelter was installed underneath the East Stand. As the War drew on, the terraces of the North Stand were piled high with sacks full of salvaged metal.

The biggest changes took place in the West Stand. Coopper was fortunate enough to retain his small office, but the rest of the stand was converted into a decontamination centre, on stand-by, to be used in the event of a chemical attack on London. Hospital beds were laid out in the restaurant, anti-gas equipment installed in the dressing rooms and the RFU Committee tearoom became a ladies' restroom.

Throughout the war, Coopper assisted where he could, and maintained the RFU's administration of the remaining schools, universities and service fixtures. He watched the stadium's deterioration and made preparations for when things would once more return to normal.

Captain Wodehouse

Like the First World War, the conflict came at a heavy price. England's first Grand Slam, back in 1913, had been secured by Capt. Norman Wodehouse. During the First World War, Wodehouse had been awarded the Albert Medal for rescuing a man overboard during the Battle of Jutland. A successful naval career had followed and he progressed to the rank of Vice-Admiral before entering the Second

World War as a Convoy Commodore. In 1941, his convoy was attacked by German submarines. Wodehouse ordered the convoy to scatter, saving many lives but not his own. In total, fourteen former England internationals were killed during the Second World War, including Prince Alexander Obolensky.

As the war wore on, the scars built up around the stadium itself. In 1944 a German V-1 bomb landed in nearby Talma Gardens, the blast from which inflicted damage on the West Stand. Night-time air-raids and anti-aircraft fire caused thousands of shells to fall in and around Twickenham, leaving the three stands of the stadium increasingly pock-marked and leaking. Although they were eventually repaired after the War, the scattered patches on the roof of the stands remained a feature of the stadium well into the 1970s.

When the war finally ended, the civil defence moved out and former staff began to return, and Coopper presented a long list of requirements to the War Damage Commission. But the RFU found themselves well down the list of priorities for national reparations. The upper tier of the West Stand, at least, would remain out of service for the immediate future.

1945

Cooper had been intending to step down as RFU secretary in 1939, but the war had extended his stay considerably. Afterwards, he was persuaded to remain in post a further year to help oversee the handover to his successor, Doug Prentice. Prentice brought his family to Twickenham, including his son Tom, who years later would provide this eyewitness account of the post-war scenes at the stadium:

No work, repairs, maintenance, paint (except grass cutting) had been possible, so one can imagine the state the place was in as the staff, one by one, began to return in 1945 and later.

Everything in the way of paint and materials were in short supply. The roofs of the stands still had holes caused by anti-aircraft shells falling from the sky as shrapnel, the iron work was rusty, the crowd barriers weakened, woodwork and seats needing repair or replacement, to name but part of the problem.

The whole of the area underneath the South Terrace (before the South Stand was built) had become seriously neglected during the War, where it housed Civil Defence vehicles, and a plague of rats had infested the area which was used for cutting up logs. Fuel was in short supply, as was every other commodity. But every kind of sports event in the country was fully booked! The people had been starved of sport and entertainment in the war years and one could be sure that stadia would be full for practically every event. It took years to get Twickenham right. The ground staff could only look after the pitch, seating and sign posting. The constructional work in those days was carried out by the Humphries Bros of London. Repair to the concrete, the holes in the roofs, drainage of the pitch, building of restaurants had to be fitted in as and when licenses for buildings and materials became available. Not until the appointment of a Clerk of Works, Mr Harold Clark, many years later, was the stadium work really put in hand.

Only those who lived through the life and death struggles of the War can recall the restrictions, rationing, controls and licenses, but although when it was all over we were left shattered and impoverished. The RFU like so many organisations gradually recovered and can be justly proud of the policies adopted at the time, and the development of the game since, what one hopes, will be the last time sport had to close down.

Victory Internationals

Rugby returned to Twickenham on 24 November 1945 with an England XV *v.* New Zealand Army side. The following year a series of *Victory Internationals* were held at Twickenham with a representative England XV defeating Ireland and Scotland, and narrowly losing to Wales. Huge crowds turned out for the games, as well as the Varsity Match and Middlesex 7s. Residents of nearby Whitton Road recall hordes of Welshmen, standing on top of the railings and all over the top of the BBC's old radio commentary box.

Twickenham Stadium, like the nation, had weathered the storm, and by 1947 the fixtures were confirmed and the Five Nations Championship was ready to return.

Left: Repaired flak holes in the roof of stand.

Above: North Stand swarf store.

Above right: England XV *v.* Scotland XV, Victory International, 1946.

Right: Repairs to the East Stand.

Grand Slammers

The RFU had recommended that the Home Nations resume relations with a reformed French Rugby Federation in 1939. The Second World War intervened, but France duly returned to the international fold in 1947. This meant that a Grand Slam might be achieved for the first time since Ronald Cove-Smith's England side had last claimed one in 1928.

No side managed it in the first season back. England shared the Championship with Wales, but lost decisively at home to an impressive Irish side that included Jackie Kyle and Karl Mullen. Ireland would pick up their first Grand Slam the following season and, enjoying their first truly dominant period in the tournament's history, claimed three Championships in four years between 1948 and 1951. England remained inconsistent and twice suffered home defeats to Wales in 1950 and 1952, as the men in red claimed Grand Slams of their own.

The 1950 clash against Wales was a particular landmark for the stadium. A record 75,500 spectators bore witness to a Lewis Jones-inspired Wales recording only their second ever victory at Twickenham.

Richmond's versatile Nim Hall had been leading the English resistance since the Victory Internationals of 1946. Inconsistency posed questions about the overall mentality and resolve of the side until salvation came in the shape of a tough-tackling, blood-and-thunder Lancastrian. Sale hooker Eric Evans made his debut in 1948, but was unable to hold down a regular place in the front row until the 1951 season. At home in Manchester he took to training with the Busby Babes at Manchester United, and thereafter quickly impressed the Twickenham faithful with his on-field rallying of the troops and acts of selfless bravery. In addition to Evans, an immensely physical wing forward, by the name of Don White, had forced his way back into the international setup after terrorising oppositions with his county side East Midlands. Hall was appointed captain in 1953, and England at last seemed to have a team that was capable of rivalling the Welsh, Irish and the rapidly improving French.

Back to Winning Ways

A narrow win in Cardiff was followed by a creditable draw in Dublin before France visited Twickenham in late February. The game saw Jeff Butterfield make his debut, and the Northampton centre marked the occasion by putting in a match-winning performance. Few players have taken to the Twickenham grass as well as Butterfield did that afternoon and it was his interception that set up a try in the first minute of the game. This gave England an early lead, with Evans adding a try of his own before half-time. Butterfield continued his all-action display in the second half and his attacking play was rewarded in the final minute of the game with a third try, securing an 11-0 win.

England went into the final match of the season, against Scotland, needing only a draw to secure the championship. In an age of low-scoring, grinding battles of attrition, the final scoreline was something to behold. Six tries and four conversions gave England a 26-8 win, an emphatic way to end an unbeaten championship.

Another successful season followed in 1954. This time only defeat to France in the final game preventing an English Grand Slam. Evans lost his place in 1955 and England stuttered but in 1956 he was made captain and ten players made their debuts in a new-look side.

Among the backs were Dickie Jeeps, a scrum-half who had been one of the stand-out performers during the 1955 British and Irish Lions tour of South Africa, and Peter Jackson an attacking winger from Coventry, who would build a reputation as the scorer of crucial tries. Alongside Evans, Northampton's Ron Jacobs earned the first of his twenty-nine caps. Behind them stood the varsity pairing of David Marques and John Currie, who forged a formidable second-row partnership that would add solidity to the English pack for the next five years.

The new-look side clicked against the Irish with Butterfield, Evans and Jackson all running-in tries, to record a 20-0 home victory. In the end they finished second in 1956, but hopes were high that they might go one better the following year.

The First Grand Slam?

The 1957 season began with England's dominant front row and general forward play securing narrow wins in both Cardiff and Dublin before the visit of the French. France were no longer the poor relations of the tournament, and had shared the Championship for the first time in 1954 and again in 1955, but the England pack were inspired once more, keeping the French at bay and allowing Jeeps to spread the ball around the backs. Jackson made the most of it by finishing off two tries in the first half. France came back with a second half-try of their own, before Evans added a third, securing a 9-5 win for the home side.

The victory meant that only Scotland stood between England and a clean sweep. In anticipation of the decisive final Test match, a reporter in *The Times* coined a new phrase to describe a team who managed to win every game of the Five Nations Championship and, for the first time, the term 'Grand Slam' entered the rugby lexicon.

Scotland had lost their previous home game to Ireland but could still secure a share of the Championship by defeating England. Once again English forward supremacy was telling and a sell-out Twickenham crowd watched the home side run in three tries to none. England had secured their first Grand Slam since 1928.

1958 was another dominant year for the men in white. Much of the same fifteen was selected and a late George Hastings penalty secured a second successive Championship. They finished the year unbeaten, despite a winter visit by the Wallabies, who provided a close, physical encounter that was only settled in the dying moments when the irrepressible Peter Jackson broke through the Australia defence to score a memorable try.

In six exceptional years, the 1950s had given England four Championship victories, including three outright and one Grand Slam.

Left: Peter Jackson.

Above: Queen Elizabeth II, England *v.* Scotland, 1957.

Above right: South Terrace, England *v.* Wales, 1952.

Above far right: Welsh supporters, 1952.

Below far right: 1940s post-war crowd.

Below right: Eric Evans, England *v.* Australia, 1958.

18

Sharp's Victory

At their thirty-second attempt, France claimed their first outright Five Nations Championship in 1959. Along with Wales, they would go on to dominate the Five Nations Championship throughout the 1960s and 1970s, but England were afforded another moment in the sun in 1963. Ron Jacobs and Peter Jackson remained from the class of '57, but the side were now captained by an exciting fly-half, from Wasps, called Richard Sharp.

The winter of 1962/63 had been the coldest on record and snow that had fallen on Boxing Day was still on the ground in March. A variety of methods were employed to try and thaw the hard Twickenham ground as the Calcutta Cup tie that would decide the championship approached.

The Richard Sharp Game

England sat on top of the table, one point clear of their opponents Scotland. Scotland could win the Championship themselves, for the first time since 1938, if they beat their hosts. But, as it turned out, the 1963 Calcutta Cup, though a close affair, was destined to go down in history as the 'Richard Sharp' game.

Scotland stormed out of the blocks, a try and a conversion setting up an eight point lead inside the first 15 minutes. This was still the era of low-scoring games and sides rarely overturned such deficits, but England composed themselves and countered in an effort to secure a foothold in the game. Towards the end of the half, their efforts were rewarded when Jackson and Sharp combined to set up a chance that was driven over by Cambridge prop, Nick Drake-Lee.

The second half will always be remembered for Sharp's try. Clarke fed him the ball from out the back of the scrum and the fly-half was running at speed before he had even collected it. Seeing a gap, he wrong footed one Scottish defender and eluded a second. The Scottish full-back was still to beat however and so Sharp made to pass but, spotting the covering run of a Scotland defender, he changed his mind and ended up inadvertently selling the full-back a dummy. Quick as a flash, Sharp was through for a stunning individual try and the English crowd were in raptures.

Some stout defending during the remainder of the game meant that England ran out 10-8 winners, securing the Championship and ensuring that Sharp's try would be the defining score of the 1963 season.

Though the England fans on the terraces couldn't have known it, fortune would dictate that 1963 would be England's last truly successful championship for quite some time. Maybe this is why English supporters of a certain age keep Sharp's try fresh in their memories and close to their hearts.

Above: M. S. Phillips, England *v.* Scotland, 1963.

Right: Richard Sharp.

ENGLAND *v* SCOTLAND

TWICKENHAM
SATURDAY 16th MARCH
1963
OFFICIAL PROGRAMME
ONE SHILLING

Above: England *v.* France, 1963.

Left: Match programme, England *v.* Scotland, 1963.

19

Streakers

For all the spectacular moments of triumph and despair played out on the Twickenham turf, for some people, a selection of the stadium's most memorable moments have of been a rather different variety.

The unusual fad of taking off all your clothes and haring around very public spaces took off initially in the 1970s and has continued to this day. Few may be aware, however, that streaking seems to have made its sporting debut at Twickenham.

In 1974, Michael O'Brien, an Australian, was apparently less concerned with a charity match between an England and France XV than he was with winning a drunken £10 bet. Shortly after accepting the bet, he was spotted 'running free' along the Twickenham touchline, with two policemen in hot pursuit. The East Stand, very much enjoying the Benny Hill-like spectacle burst out laughing when PC Perry, upon apprehending him, did the honourable thing by shielding O'Brien's manhood behind his policeman's helmet. O'Brien was taken down to the local station and aptly fined £10 for his part in the disturbance. A subsequent photograph of the incident won 'Photograph of the Year' in *Life* magazine.

Though O'Brien was the first, he is not the most fondly remembered Twickenham streaker. That accolade lies with a certain Miss Erica Roe. Roe chose half-time in a test-match between England and Australia in 1982 to burst onto the international scene. England captain Bill Beaumont was annoyed to discover that his teammates were paying no attention to his half-time team talk when Steve Smith informed him, 'Bill, there's a bird just run on with your bum on her chest!'

Miss Roe inspired all sorts of non-rugby related thoughts in the minds of the watching faithful, some of whom are still singing songs and writing poetry about her to this day.

Michael O'Brien, England XV v.
France XV, 1974.

20

Royals

There is at least one full England international within the royal family in the shape of Mike Tindall. But the royal association with the sport predates his marriage to Zara Phillips in 2011, and can be traced back at least as far as the opening international game at Twickenham Stadium. In attendance that day was the Prince of Wales and soon-to-be King George V, Zara's great-great-grandfather.

George V was a regular at Twickenham from 1910, right up until his death in 1936, and frequently brought his two sons with him, the future Edward VIII and George VI. In 1923, he even sent a personal note to RFU stalwart Charles Marriot to wish him a happy retirement.

Until 1995, the Royal Box was nothing more than a concrete terrace with space for twenty oak-wood chairs that were removed from Rugby Lodge/House on matchdays. Since its redevelopment in 1995, the West Stand has had a royal enclosure in the middle of the lower tier, with seats for around 300 people. From here, in 2015, the Webb Ellis Cup will be awarded at the stadium for a second time.

Queen Elizabeth II has been a frequent visitor to the stadium, perhaps most memorably when she awarded the Webb Ellis Cup to the Australian captain, Nick Farr-Jones, after the final of the 1991 World Cup.

Both Prince William and Prince Harry are avid rugby fans, who attend games at Twickenham whenever their schedules allow, but they rarely sit inside the Royal Box. A strict dresscode is maintained at all times and the Princes, who prefer to sport their colours, sit alongside the players' wives and families instead.

Above: Prince Charles meets injured troops, Help for Heroes charity match, March 2008.

Above right: England XV *v.* Presidents XV, 1971.

Below right: Lord Wakefield and Princess Elizabeth, Middlesex 7s, 1951.

Left: Prince Chichibu, 1937.

Prince William and Prince Harry, 2010.

21

The Welsh Wizards

The post-Sharp 1960s and 1970s were a fallow time for English rugby. It wasn't that the red rose didn't produce good players: the likes of Bob Hiller, Roger Uttley, Fran Cotton, John Pullin, Peter Wheeler, David Duckham and Bill Beaumont all did their bit for their country during these years, but England couldn't seem to get enough of them on the pitch at the same time to challenge the dominant French and Welsh sides.

An unprecedented five-way share of the 1973 Championship, when every side won their two home games and lost their two away games was a rare bright spot, of sorts, even if it was sandwiched in between four consecutive bottom place finishes.

England's biggest problem during this time was the standard of the opposition. France had finally secured their first Grand Slam in 1968 before, in typical French style, failing to record a single victory the following year. Despite this, France have remained serious championship contenders ever since and recorded the unique achievement of winning a Grand Slam with the same fifteen players featuring in every match in 1977.

The Prince of Wales

In 1967, a young scrum-half by the name of Gareth Edwards made his debut for Wales. The following year he scored his first try in an 11-11 draw against England at Twickenham. His midfield partnerships with Barry John and Phil Bennett were the catalyst for the success of a Welsh side, further bolstered by the likes of Mervyn Davies, J. P. R. Williams, Gerald Davies, Graham Price and Bobby Windsor. This extraordinary group of talented players would win shares of eight Championships in eleven seasons, including six outright victories and three Grand Slams.

During the 1978 season, Edwards would earn his fiftieth cap in front of the watching faithful at Twickenham. As the Welsh team ran out, their captain, Phil Bennett, instructed his teammates to hold back, allowing Edwards to unwittingly take to the field by himself. English and Welsh fans alike rose as one to salute one of the finest rugby players to have taken to the Twickenham field.

The Men Who Made Twickenham: No. 3 — Harold Clark

Harold Clark applied for the job of foreman at the Twickenham Stadium in 1964. After impressing at the interview, he was offered the job but refused it. Questioned as to why, he replied that he would only join as 'Clerk of Works'.

The RFU agreed to the demand and Clark was shown around the place. Moments later, upon allegedly discovering the majority of his staff of twelve either drunk or asleep underneath the South Terrace, he resigned.

Eventually matters were ironed out and Clark was given complete control of operational matters. For the next eighteen years he would be the stadium's eyes and ears. In that time, he succeeded in transforming a stadium that had never really recovered from the Second World War, into a tightly-run ship.

One of his first acts was to clear out rubbish that had been steadily accumulating under the North Stand, converting the space into a series of workshops. Inside these he housed his staff of plumbers, joiners, engineers and painters, employed as replacements for the casual staff that had formerly been in place.

He then introduced a pitch innovation called sandbanding, which compensated for an over-compressed pitch and allowed the surface to drain. The technique was a success and widely copied in other sports stadiums for many years.

Clark oversaw the reroofing of the East and West Stands in 1971 that resulted in the 'R. F. U. TWICKENHAM' lettering that would subsequently feature on the roof of the stands.

In 1974, it became a requirement for sports stadiums to obtain licenses. Clark made the necessary alterations and Twickenham Stadium received license No. 001, as the first stadium in the country to make the grade.

Howard Clark made a significant contribution to the professionalisation of ground works and maintenance around the stadium and, although the stadium no longer employs a clerk of works, his work has since been continued by a large team of professional craftspeople.

Above: Gareth Edwards, England *v.* Wales, 1968.

Right: Twickenham, 1970.

Left: Welsh fans, 1968.

Above: East Stand during reroofing, 1971.

Left: Harold Clark.

22

Lions

The British and Irish Lions are one of rugby's most noble traditions. But on only one occasion have the tourists visited the English national stadium and, when it happened, it was by royal decree.

The 1970s represents one of the high-water marks in Lions history. Barry John had kicked the side to a series win against New Zealand in 1971 and Willie John McBride had captained an undefeated tour and 3-0 series victory against South Africa in 1974. In 1977, three weeks after returning from New Zealand, the Lions were called into action to play against the Barbarians, as part of the run-up to Queen Elizabeth II's Silver Jubilee celebrations.

The Barbarians, containing the likes of J. P. R. Williams, Gareth Edwards and Gerald Davies, might have been have been considered a Lions Mark II, had they not been bolstered from across the channel by the likes of J. P. Rives and J. C. Skrela.

A crowd of 58,000 watched the Lions notch up a 15-0 first-half lead. The second half was closer, but the Lions ran out 23-14 winners and over £100,000 was raised for the jubilee fund.

Above: England and Wales *v.* Ireland and Scotland, 1959.

Left: British and Irish Lions dressing room sign.

Phil Bennet and Prince Charles, British and Irish Lions *v.* Barbarians, 1977.

Invitation Only

One-off fixtures have featured at Twickenham Stadium for many years. Here are some of the most memorable:

1929 England/Wales *v.* Scotland/Ireland
Played after the unveiling of the memorial gates in honour of George Rowland Hill.

1959 England/Wales *v.* Scotland/Ireland
Jubilee match played in celebration of Twickenham Stadium's fiftieth anniversary.

1970 England/Wales *v.* Scotland/Ireland
Played to celebrate the RFU's centenary.

1971 President's XV *v.* England
Played to celebrate the RFU's centenary.

1984 England *v.* Presidents XV
Played to celebrate Twickenham's seventy-fifth anniversary.

1986 Overseas Union *v.* Five Nations XV
Played in celebration of the IRB's centenary.

1990 Four Home Unions *v.* Rest of Europe
Fundraiser for the aftermath of the Romanian Revolution.

1996 Bath *v.* Wigan
The return leg, played under union rules, of a contest to determine England's best cross-code rugby side.

2005 North *v.* South
Played to raise funds for the victims of the South-East Asian tsunami.

2011 North *v.* South
Played to raise funds for the Help For Heroes charity in support of injured servicemen.

23

Forward Dominance

Many English rugby fans were not unhappy to see the back of the 1970s. Despite contributing some very good players to several successful Lions tours, England had never quite managed to field a team that could match the Welsh and French, who had dominated the tournament since the late 1950s. By the time the 1980 Five Nations Championship rolled around, England had gone seventeen years without an outright championship victory and six years without beating Wales, statistics unseen since pre-Twickenham days.

In a further echo of the past, the 1979 season had delivered England their biggest defeat against Wales since 1905. However, despite eventually finishing second bottom of the table, they had actually gone into that final game against Wales with an outside chance of earning a share of the championship. This was thanks in no small part to the efforts of their captain.

Bill Beaumont was another tough-tackling, no-nonsense Lancastrian, very much in the Eric Evans mould and, those that remembered Evans, hoped that the second-row forward might be the man who could finally draw England out of their stupor.

Forward Dominance

Fortunately for Beaumont, he would line up for the 1980 Five Nations campaign behind a front row trio of Peter Wheeler, the Leicester Tigers' captain, Gloucester's uncapped Phil Blakeway and veteran dog-of-war Fran Cotton, recalled for his twenty-seventh cap. Alongside him, for the most part, was Maurice Colclough. This formidable front five was the platform upon which England hoped to build their campaign. Among the backs, Leicester Tigers' duo Clive Woodward and Paul Dodge were ready to provide the creative spark at centre, while full-back Dusty Hare kicked the points.

Forward dominance and set-piece mastery allowed England to rack-up twenty-four points against Ireland, who could supply only nine in return at the opening fixture at Twickenham. Paris was next, a place where England hadn't beaten France since 1964. But this time was different. Once again, the tight-five turned the screw, subjecting the French pack to enormous pressure that resulted in a 13-17 win for the visitors.

Taming of the Dragon

The result in Paris set up a home show down with Wales. Like England, Wales had won both of their opening games and results elsewhere meant that the winners of the game would almost certainly win the championship. The press utilised all of their dark arts to whip up a foul mood in the run-up to the game and, prior to kick-off, a pensive nervousness pervaded an English crowd that had grown used to Welsh victories. The feeling only intensified during the course of a low-scoring nail-biter of a game in which the lead exchanged hands no fewer than five times.

A full-blooded, bruising opening led to Welsh flanker Paul Ringer becoming the first player to be sent off at Twickenham since Cyril Brownlie, for a late tackle on John Horton that allowed Hare to kick England into a three point lead. Enraged, the Welsh struck back with an unconverted try to lead 3-4 at half-time. The men in red maintained their slender advantage until the 68th minute when Hare calmly kicked England back in front. With just 3 minutes remaining, Rees burst over the line to score what most expected to be a match-winning and possibly championship-winning try.

The 80-minute-mark passed with Wales leading 6-8. It seemed that normal service had resumed. But Billy Beaumont didn't see it that way and continued to drive his men onwards. Deep into injury-time incessant English pressure brought them another penalty. Most English supporters couldn't bear to watch, but Dusty Hare was unflappable, coolly kicking his third penalty to give England a memorable 9-8 victory.

The English pack was equally dominant in the final test at Murrayfield, and so too was Clive Woodward, who helped set up a 19-3 half-time lead. From this point on, the Grand Slam was never in doubt. England eventually won 30-18 and claimed their first Grand Slam since 1958.

The 1980 success was celebrated deep into the decade and, magnificent as it was, in the end, it did not prove to be the immediate catalyst for more fruitful years. New faces and a new team would be required for that.

Above: Twickenham Stadium, 1980s.

Right: Bill Beaumont, 1980.

Left: Match ticket, England *v.* Wales, 1980.

24

The Long Forgotten South Stand

The fabled and mostly unrealised South Stand represents the longest running construction saga in the history of Twickenham Stadium and harks back to another of the reasons that the site may have been deemed unsuitable back in 1907. Back then, although the stadium was surrounded on all sides by green tracts of land, a row of Victorian villas lay alongside Whitton Road up to the corner of Oak Lane.

Various extensions to the South Terrace brought it within spitting distance of the back gardens of these houses and so 170–226 Whitton Road began to loom ever larger in the minds of those who wished to extend the ground southwards. Since 1925 the South Terrace had been the only uncovered side of the stadium. The means and desire to invest in a fourth stand had always been there but unfortunately so had the houses.

Rugby Houses

On the corner, where Whitton Road met Oak Lane, stood a large eighteenth-century residence. It had originally been called The Laurels but had been renamed Vanda Lodge, after the type of apple that once grew where the east stand now stands. The RFU purchased it in 1913 and renamed it Rugby Lodge and then Rugby House.

In 1925, Assistant-Secretary Jack Langley discovered the flood damaged property to be in a poor state and moved his family to 216 Whitton Road. The old lodge was pulled down and 216 became the second 'Rugby House', with Charles Marriot's office occupying a quarter of the ground floor.

So the RFU owned one of the houses behind the South Terrace but that didn't mean that the other residents would allow them to build a new stand on top of their flower beds. This was the summary that was presented to Honorary Secretary Bill Ramsay when he tentatively broached the subject in 1949.

Putting all thoughts of major development aside, Ramsay instead decided to remove the iconic South Terrace clock tower and replace it with an equally iconic weathervane of Hermes passing a rugby ball. The weathervane, now mounted high above the East-Stand, would become the image that greeted television viewers at the start of Twickenham broadcasts for years to come.

Spiralling Costs

The need for a South Stand was therefore shelved but not forgotten and in 1964 architects estimated the costs of a new stand to be around £225,000. Planning permission was sought and rejected. Whitton Road residents were not willing to give up their gardens or sunlight and a subsequent enquiry made clear that permission would not be given unless the RFU acquired another three of the eight most affected properties.

The RFU set about doing precisely that and by 1968 had purchased enough of them to satisfy the Minister for Housing. Another construction quote was arranged but this time the costs were estimated at a prohibitive £620,000. With much muttering and shaking of heads, the plans were put back on the shelf.

History has shown that the RFU thrives when electing to invest in its stadium. 1968 was an opportunity missed, and costs rocketed over the following decade. By the end of 1978, it was estimated that the now fabled South Stand would incur costs of over £2 million. But the need remained and in the end a solution was arrived at that satisfied few and pleased none.

A cost-effective, off-the-shelf solution was proposed. The RFU could make significant savings on architect's fees by replicating an existing stand at nearby Goodwood. It would seat over 5,000 and had standing room for a further 6,000. But from the outset it was not welcomed, and more than one insider commented that it was considerably better suited to a racecourse than a rugby stadium.

Nevertheless work was begun in 1980 and, by 1981, a conspicuously modern South Stand had taken residence where the South Terrace had long stood. The contrast between the new stand and those that were built in the 1920s and 1930s was marked. Furthermore, for the first time, Twickenham had a small number of corporate boxes and hospitality suites.

A Brave New World

This prompted some soul searching within an organisation that remained amateur and proud but Britain was changing. Corporate hospitality was very much the shape of things to come and in time the RFU would discover that it was uniquely placed to benefit. A spacious function room, christened the Rose Room, filled out much of the South Stand interior and the stadium's first rugby museum was installed alongside it.

Although it had been a long time coming, the 'old' new south stand was destined to be unloved. Ultimately it would stand for less time than it had taken to get planning permission to build.

Cleared South Terrace, 1980.

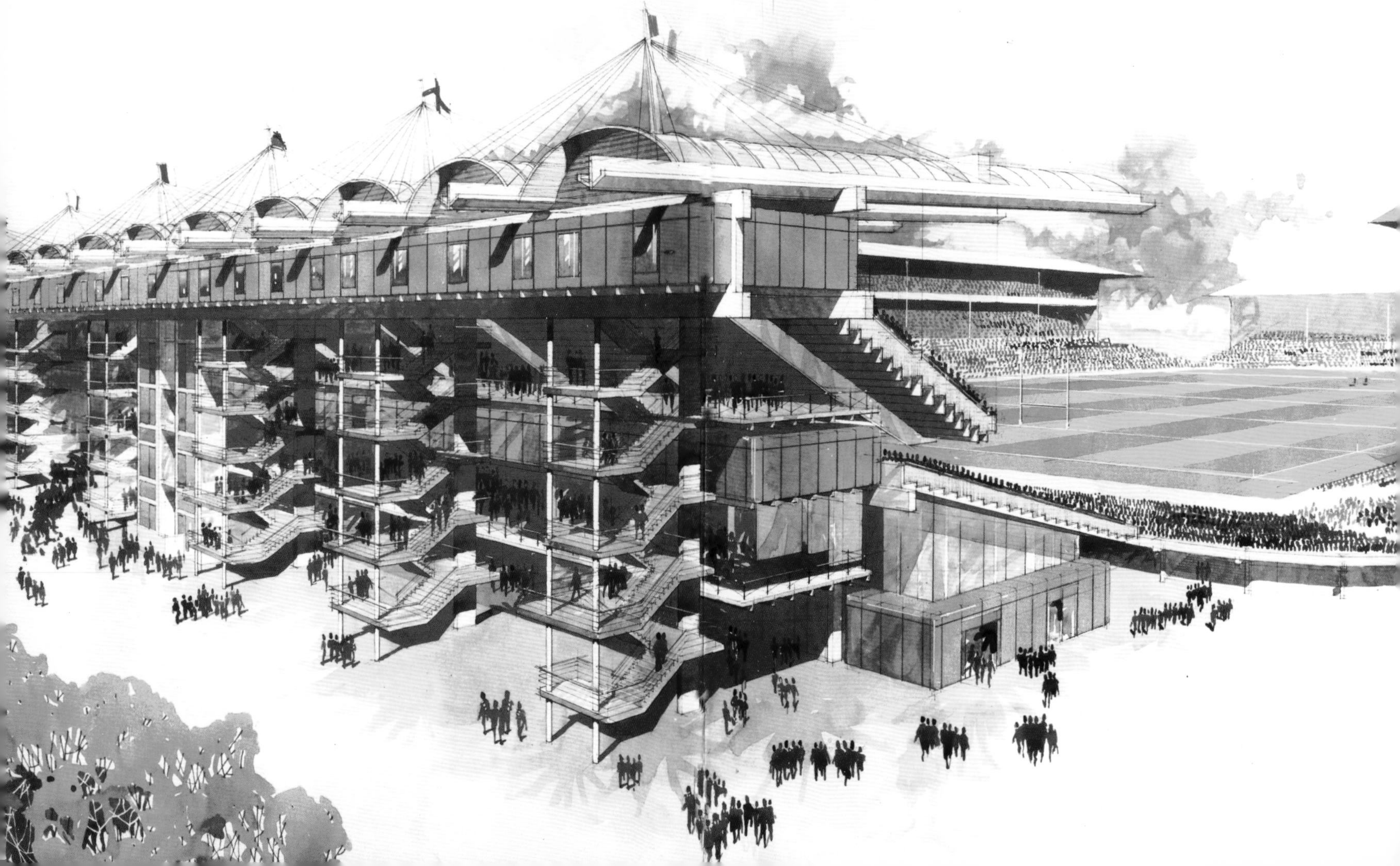

Right: Housing to the south, 1940s.

Left: Architect's plans, 1979.

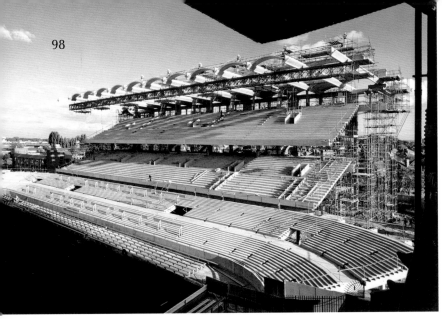

Above: Twickenham Stadium, *c.* 1981.

Above left: New South Stand.

Left: South Stand corporate box, 1980.

25

A Stadium For All

'Anyone can play on my pitch.'

Head Groundsman Keith Kent

The County Championship

The County Championship has been running since 1889, and is therefore the oldest RFU-run competition, outside of the international tests. Initially, the format of the competition was such that one of the finalists went into the competition decider as the 'home' team, and so it was only when Middlesex earned this distinction that the final was held at Twickenham Stadium.

This all changed in 1984 when a decision was taken for the stadium to be used as the venue for all future finals. Lancashire are the competition's most successful team and the popularity of the competition has ebbed and flowed over the years.

One memorable high came in 1991, when Cornwall and Yorkshire played out a final in front of 55,000 spectators. Yorkshire took a 16-3 lead, but in a thrilling encounter Cornwall pegged them back to 16-16, forcing the game into extra time. In extra time, 'Trelawny' rang out as the Duchy took control to run out 29-20 winners.

The RFU Club Competition

The RFU Club Competition didn't come into being until 1972 and, after undergoing a string of name-changes and makeovers, came to be known as the Anglo-Welsh Cup. For many years, the final was held at Twickenham Stadium and though the tournament was eventually superseded by more prestigious club competitions, such as the Premiership and European Finals, it was the RFU Cup that first established the stadium as a venue for club finals.

The Premiership

League competitions were not introduced in England until 1987 and, during the 2000/01 season, an innovation was introduced that brought the competition to Twickenham Stadium. The top four teams in the final table would contest two semi-finals, with the winners meeting in a final at Twickenham. From 2003 onwards, the play-off final would become the championship decider.

The 2008 Premiership final would herald the swansong for one of English rugby's greatest ever performers. Lawrence Dallaglio had helped England to a second successive World Cup Final at the start of the season, but had returned to his club side, London Wasps, to find them languishing near the foot of the table. A remarkable string of results followed, culminating in Wasps defeating Leicester Tigers 20-16 at Twickenham in May. A sell-out 81,600 crowd gave Dallaglio a standing ovation as he left the field in the 67th minute. The fixture has sold out for every subsequent play-off final since as the concept has taken hold in the minds of English rugby fans.

The European Cup

The European club rugby competition had been set up in 1995 and quickly became acknowledged as one of the most prestigious competitions in club rugby. English sides have never lost a European Final at Twickenham. Northampton Saints won there in 2000 and London Wasps won there twice in 2004 and 2007.

The Schools Final

As well as elite clubs and counties, universities and schools regularly host their tournament finals at HQ. The schools tournament began for under-15s in 1988 and under-18s in 1991 and has a proven track record for blooding future England internationals. Mike Tindall, Matthew Tait, James Haskell, Danny Care, Elliot Daly, Charlie Walker and Marlon Yarde are just a handful of players to have featured in the final over the years.

In 2013, the final was switched from midweek to Saturday afternoon, enabling an increase in attendance to over 10,000. This figure is expected to increase over the coming years as the contest continues to grow in popularity.

Pitch Maintenance

Excavated soil from an extension to the Metropolitan underground line was used to raise the pitch level to alleviate the risk of flooding when the site was first developed back in 1907. The RFU then approached a Mr Charlie Hale, who was appointed Groundsman and took up residence in the Cottage, after it had been built in 1908.

In 1909, George Street of Blackheath was approached by the RFU to assist in laying the pitch, and Hale took the decision to keep the grass long as the best means of protection.

Throughout the history of the stadium, the people charged with maintaining the playing surface have faced the challenge of frozen winter pitches. For many years, Hale, who retired in 1946, and his sons would lay straw on the surface of the field, to be removed before kick-off as the best form of insulation. This method continued up until the 1950s when futuristic space heaters, resembling giant hair dryers, were used on the pitch, as well as straw.

In 1964, Howard Clark refused the position of foreman and instead was appointed clerk of works. As part of the role, he took responsibility for the pitch and introduced the technique of sandbanding to help drain the pitch and alleviate against ground frost. The method was successful and widely copied elsewhere.

In 2002, Keith Kent was appointed head groundsman, a position that he had previously held at Old Trafford. Since then, he has introduced a number of innovations that have significantly improved the Twickenham playing surface. Most visible are the giant lighting rigs that are wheeled onto the grass during the winter months to allow the grass to grow and guard against the frost. Additionally, in 2012, a process of hybridisation was introduced that rendered the pitch 3 per cent artificial. Gone are the days of the Twickenham mudbath!

Above: Lymm High School under-15s, 2010.

Right: Straw pitch insulation, 1932.

Above: Pitch lights, 2009.

Above right: Space heaters, 1950s.

Right: Wilmslow High School *v.* Wellington College under-15s final, 2010.

Left: University and College finals, 2011.

Brighton College under-15s, 2010.

26

Last Great Amateurs

The 1980s began with a Grand Slam, followed by two second place finishes, but England would spend most of the rest of the decade hovering around the foot of the Five Nations Championship table. From 1984 onwards, the side began to collect a rare crop of players who would far surpass the ordinary.

Cyril Lowe, the original flying-winger, had remained England's record tryscorer since hanging up his boots way back in 1923. Sixty years on, his true successor was found at last.

Like Lowe, Rory Underwood was a fighter pilot and a prodigious tryscorer, with the ability to elude defenders with his speed of thought and rapid acceleration. He made his full debut at Twickenham in 1984, and scored his first try the following month against France. It was the first of forty-nine in a career that would span thirteen seasons.

A new half-back combination in the form of Bath's scrum-half Richard Hill and fly-half Rob Andrew broke into the side over the 1984 and 1985 seasons. Andrew, who played for Nottingham, Wasps and Newcastle Falcons, had an exceptional right boot and his accurate place-kicking and dropped goals would become a feature of the English game for ten consecutive seasons.

England, however, remained in transition and a poor 1987 season, where they finished bottom of the championship table, precipitated a further clearing of the decks. Inside-centre Will Carling made his debut against France in 1988 at the age of twenty-two. His field presence and leadership qualities were apparent to all and, by the end of the year he had been installed as England's youngest ever captain.

The following year, an outside-centre from Bath, called Jeremy Guscott, made his debut. In Carling and Guscott, England had unearthed what would become a truly outstanding centre partnership. Natural, attacking footballers blessed with pace, which Carling allied to power and Guscott to running guile. It was no coincidence that the side's fortunes began to improve as these two players developed a deeper understanding of the other's game.

As the backs improved so too did the pack. Combative hooker Brian Moore earned the first of his sixty-four caps against Scotland in 1987. Backing him up was the long arm of the law in the shape of Preston Grasshopper's Wade Dooley and Harlequins' Paul Ackford, whose second-row partnership was supported by Leicester Tiger's Dean Richards who held things together at No. 8 – three serving policemen, three formidable rugby players.

'Swing Low, Sweet Chariot…'

It was hoped that 1988 would be the season that 'plodding and predictable' England finally turned the corner, but straight defeats against France and Wales suggested otherwise. A scrappy away win against Scotland returned the Calcutta Cup, leaving only Ireland at Twickenham. With nothing much to play for, few expected fireworks. The Irish had been enjoying their best decade since the 1940s and went in at the break leading 0-3. An injury to the English captain Nigel Melville made matters worse, and despondency began to set in among the long suffering faithful. Little did they know that they were about to bear witness to beginning of a new chapter in the long and illustrious history of Twickenham Stadium and English rugby.

In the second half, England ran riot by scoring six unanswered tries. Rory Underwood claimed two, Gary Rees another and Chris Oti, making only his second international appearance, scored three. In homage to his feats, the English crowd began a spontaneous rendition of 'Swing Low Sweet Chariot', an African-American spiritual song that had been an English clubhouse favourite for some time. Exactly what the English fans were getting at can never be properly established, but what is unquestionable is on that March afternoon, English rugby found its most enduring anthem. The 35-3 victory represented the biggest championship victory ever recorded.

Prior to this game, England had been plodding, predictable and perennial underachievers. After the game they were the rising force in world rugby and threatened to carry all before them.

Carling captained them to an impressive win over a very strong Australian side later that year, and they finished the 1989 Five Nations Championship in second place, having defeated eventual winners France by 11-0 at Twickenham. They were that close, could 1990 be their year?

The Slow Walk to Victory…

It started well. A display of open, attacking rugby, of which Adrian Stoop would have been proud, brought about four tries at home to Ireland. This was followed by hugely impressive wins in Paris and against Wales at Twickenham, which caused the press to herald some of the best English rugby in living memory. But, amidst all the euphoria, few had noticed that England's final opponents Scotland, had quietly gone about racking up three wins of their own. Murrayfield would play host to a game that would settle the Calcutta Cup, Triple Crown, Five Nations Championship and a Grand Slam.

England were narrow favourites, but from the moment David Sole slow-walked his side into the seething Murrayfield cauldron, the psychological upper hand lay with the Scots. 1990 was Scotland's year and England were sent home to lick their wounds and reflect upon what might have been. It was a crushing disappointment for what was a very young team, and English fans might have been forgiven for thinking 'same old, same old'. But if they did they were wrong. Will Carling's team learned from their disappointment and to their eternal credit used the defeat as a catalyst to spur them on to the most successful period in English rugby since the 1920s.

Towards the end of 1990, Brain Moore and Jeff Probyn were joined in the front row by England's youngest-ever prop forward, Barking's Jason Leonard. Leonard's career would span fifteen years, including two world cup finals and a record 114 caps. Dooley and Ackford operated the second row and, behind them, Richards had Mike Teague and Peter Winterbottom in support. It seemed England had assembled a pack that could turn the screw like the class of 1980. Chastened by the disappointment of Murrayfield, this was an approach that team manager Geoff Cooke was keen to exploit. And so, contrary to the attacking verve, that had so captivated the press in 1990, the following year England would emulate the class of 1980 and indeed 1957, adopting a safety-first game that relied on forward pressure and penalties.

Comfortable wins were secured against Ireland and Wales, either side of England taking their revenge on the Scots by beating them 21-12 at Twickenham. Just as it had done in 1990, the 1991 championship came down to a final game shoot-out between two teams. This time, unbeaten France would be England's opponents but crucially, with the experience of last year's disappointment fresh in their memory, things would be settled at Twickenham.

Le Crunch

The giant new North Stand towered over the other three sides of the stadium as 61,000 fans prepared for a game that will now be forever referred to as 'Le Crunch'. England, cautious that history should not be repeated, flew out of the blocks and took an early lead. But then the French did what the French do. England kicked a penalty wide and, on receiving the ball behind his own try line, Serge Blanco chose not to kick but to run. The ball progressed down the right flank where Didier Camberabero chipped into his own hands, before releasing Philippe Saint-Andre to score a try that was later voted the greatest-ever scored at the stadium.

It was a try worthy of a Grand Slam, but this time England would not yield. An Underwood try and several more kicks established an 18-9 advantage, before the obstinate French hit back with two second half tries of their own. With little now between the two sides, England were in real danger of squandering a second successive Slam. France threw everything at them for the remainder of the match, but England's defence remained strong, holding out for a 21-19 victory. When the final whistle blew, fans invaded the pitch once more, as they had done in 1910. But this time it was Will Carling, Rob Andrew and Rory Underwood's turn to be carried from the pitch. England had their first Grand Slam in eleven years.

Back-to-Back Slams?

The 1991 World Cup may have left a bittersweet taste in their mouths but the English team were in no mood to relinquish their Five Nations crown at the start of the 1992 season. This time there would be no need for a Grand Slam decider, England were unbeatable and completed their most dominant season since 1924 by smashing the Welsh 24-0 at Twickenham. It was the first time any side had completed back-to-back Grand Slams since Davies' and Wakefield's heroes of the 1920s.

In a tradition that has now become embedded in the rugby calendar Twickenham welcomed southern hemisphere opposition in the autumn of 1992 and 1993. South Africa, recently re-admitted to the fold, arrived first and played out a high scoring game which England won 33-16, despite trailing at half-time. The following year, New Zealand arrived and were defeated 16-9 in front of the newly rebuilt East Stand. It seemed that modern Twickenham was taking shape around a team capable of defeating the very best sides in the world.

England might have had a third Slam in four seasons in 1994 but for a brilliant solo try by Irishman Simon Geoghegan, which gave Ireland a 12-13 victory at Twickenham. Geoff Cooke, who is credited with having led England out of the wilderness, stepped down as Team Manager at the end of 1994 to be replaced by Jack Rowell as England entered a period of rebuilding.

Crossroads

Richard Hill, Jeff Probyn and Wade Dooley had all called it a day and in their place came a new crop of outstanding performers. Leicester Tiger's Martin Johnson and Martin Bayfield of Northampton Saints established a formidable second row, and Neil Back and Mike Catt made their full-test debuts. Later in their careers these players would form the core of another great England side but in 1995, World Cup year, they overlapped with an earlier generation that included Carling, Guscott, Andrew and Underwood and between them conjured up another memorable achievement.

Improbably a third Grand Slam show-down in six seasons saw England and Scotland settle the honours in the last round of fixtures, as they had done in 1990. This time, like in 1992, things would be decided at Twickenham. The West Stand was a building site that year, no tries were scored but Rob Andrew's boot ensured that England triumphed. It was England's third Grand Slam in five seasons.

France put paid to English hopes of a repeat in the first round of the 1996 season but England rallied to secure the Triple Crown and retain the Championship, which in the event of a tie was now being decided on goal-difference. Captain Will Carling had announced before the game that it would be his last. As he left the field, Twickenham stood as one to salute the most successful captain in English history.

Carling drew the curtain on what was the most successful period for English rugby since the 1920s. Since losing out to Scotland in 1990, England had bounced back by winning outright four of the next six Championships, including three Grand Slams, and history records that it would be Carling's side who would be remembered as the last truly great side of the amateur age.

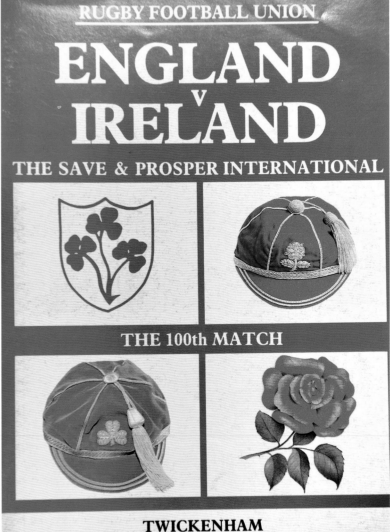

RUGBY FOOTBALL UNION

ENGLAND
v
IRELAND

THE SAVE & PROSPER INTERNATIONAL

THE 100th MATCH

**TWICKENHAM
SATURDAY 19th MARCH 1988**

OFFICIAL
PROGRAMME
£1·00
(Including 20p

Secretary R.F.U

England dressing room.

27

The 1991 Rugby World Cup

Eighty-one years after Twickenham Stadium had permanently altered the course of English rugby, it would play host to a tournament that would permanently alter the course of world rugby.

Twickenham had already hosted a world XV-a-side tournament in the shape of the King's Cup back in 1919. But the Rugby World Cup was the first tournament that could lay claim to being a truly inclusive global international XV-a-side competition.

The notion had been first proposed to the IRB as far back as 1958 but had been rejected. In the 1980s, another concerted effort was made and, despite an initial split decision, the motion was passed.

But factions within the game remained hostile to a tournament that many believed would hasten the onset of professionalism. The inaugural 1987 tournament, co-hosted by New Zealand and Australia, was resisted to the point that international broadcasting rights were not even made available.

The tournament, however, was a triumph of will, proving to the world that it *could* be done. In addition, the IRB found themselves £2.2 million in the black and were able to distribute the sum among competing nations. The benefits of the tournament were becoming clear. Income from subsequent tournaments would be invested by the IRB in developing rugby nations. This, allied to the increased media exposure generated by the tournament, triggered a period of prolonged growth in the sport around the world.

Twickenham on the World Stage

In 1987, the tournament only needed to take place to be considered a success. The second tournament, however, would be judged by a far stricter set of criteria. And the responsibility fell on England and Twickenham Stadium as hosts.

It was hoped that live satellite television broadcasting would bring the event to a global audience for the first time. This was seen as the key to ensuring that the tournament was commercially successful. But all of this was of less concern to English rugby fans, who above all wanted to see evidence that *their* side could compete against the best sides in the world and win.

The omens were good. Over seventy countries secured television rights to the tournament. The game would receive truly global media exposure, with some estimating a potential audience of over 1.5 billion. In light of this, conservative estimates predicted a return in excess of £20 million.

The England team, too, seemed also to be playing their part. Will Carling's side had secured their first Grand Slam in eleven years earlier that year, and it was hoped that the home stadium would provide a significant advantage going into the tournament. The only snag was that their opening-day opponents were reigning world champions New Zealand.

Contenders

New Zealand and Australia were regarded by many as the two best sides in the world, but the home side had beaten the Wallabies at home in 1988 and knew that if they could beat the All Blacks, they could probably beat anyone. The media build-up was frenetic. Anticipation grew as the tournament approached and, after the tournament's opening ceremony was concluded, rugby fans couldn't wait to get on with the real business of playing rugby.

A tense first half, dominated by forward play, saw England go in at half-time leading 12-9. But a break-away try, early in the second, set up a 12-16 lead for the visitors, and a platform from which they could execute their game plan. Wily and experienced, the All Blacks skilfully played the percentages, encouraging line-outs and retaining possession. For all of England's forward prowess and attacking back play, they could do nothing without the ball. New Zealand closed out a tactical game to win 12-16.

If this knocked the wind out of English sails, the subsequent wins for Australia, France, Italy, Scotland, Ireland and Western Samoa against Wales meant that the tournament quickly told a hold of the public's imagination.

Italy won their opening game against the USA, and England went into their game against the Azzurri several points behind them in the pool. The Italians set out to spoil England's game and prevent them from playing any kind of running game. It didn't work and instead they gave away an outrageous thirty-seven penalties, which full-back Jonathan Webb gratefully accepted and used to set an English international record by scoring twenty-four points. Although England came out 36-6 winners, it was a disappointing spectacle for the fans.

Only the USA now stood between England and the quarter-finals. 60,000 turned out to watch what was expected to be a walkover, and while England didn't play particularly well, they got the job done by winning 37-9.

Home Advantage?

As the tournament entered the knock-out rounds, the spotlight moved away from Twickenham Stadium, whose one remaining game would be the final itself. England had failed to impress in any of their pool games, and privately many believed there was little chance that they would return.

Despite being a home tournament for the English, the format meant that France would play all of their pool games and their quarter-final in front of their own fans. As luck would have it, France's quarter-final opponents in Paris turned out to be England. With questions being asked of the tournament organisers, England rolled up at the Parc de Princes with many believing it would be a bridge too far for the faltering side. England had beaten France twice in two years by starving them of ball and squeezing the life out of the French resistance. Would a similar performance show the world what they were really capable of?

Legendary French full-back Serge Blanco had announced before the tournament that the World Cup would be his international swansong. For more than a decade, he had lit up the international stage with his unpredictable, attacking back play. If England were to triumph, they would have to stop Serge.

Once more England looked to their pack. Smothering their opponents and dominating possession with the ten-man game they attempted to keep the dangerous French players from the ball. It worked. Carling, Guscott and Underwood combined to give England a try in the first half, before France pulled one back in the second. With only six minutes remaining, the scores were locked at 10-10, but in the end constant English pressure proved too much for the French who gave away a penalty before allowing Carling in for another English try. The final score was 19-10 to the visitors and England had reached the semi-finals.

If France had been fortunate enough to play all of their 1991 World Cup games on home soil, Scotland had repeated that trick and now had a Murrayfield semi-final against host nation England to look forward to. With home advantage, the Scots were slight favourites, but England were confident that they had hit on the winning formula and so employed the same possession and kicking game.

Like the French, the Scots were stifled, but so too were the English backs. With just 18 minutes remaining and the scores at 6-6, Scotland were awarded a penalty. With the game there for the taking the Scottish captain Gavin Hastings stepped up and somehow missed. With the home fans still reeling, it was Rob Andrew of England who, with just 6 minutes remaining, landed a drop-kick to give his side a 9-6 victory.

Final Plans

Three weeks after defeating the USA, England had improbably made it back to Twickenham to contest their first World Cup Final. A safety first game plan had facilitated their progress, but in the week leading up to the game, Australian wing David Campese, the tournament's stand-out performer so far, called on the English side to abandon the negative tactics that had served them so well. It may have been a calculated ploy on Campese's behalf, but sections of the English press agreed that England would need more than negative tactics to defeat Australia.

More than eighty years since the stadium had been derided for having grass that was 'too long for rugby', it was hosting a World Cup Final and all of the best Twickenham traditions were in evidence on the day of the match. In the West car park, champagne, smoked salmon and caviar were served out of the boots of Jaguars, Bentleys and Rollers. Celebrity faces from all over the world were paraded in front of television crews, speaking a dozen different languages. Under the brick façade of the old West Stand, Prince Edward and Princess Margaret were in attendance as Queen Elizabeth II was formally welcomed and shown into the same rooms that her grandfather had rested in many years before. 56,000 was the number on the gate, but some were estimating that the as many as 2 billion people around the globe would be watching. The grass had been cut to less than an inch.

There were nerves in the stands and on the field as the whistle blew and the game began. As usual, the English pack started well, but it soon became clear that they were not set up to smother the opposition with quite the vigilance of their previous two games. Andrew repeatedly chose to spread the ball out, and both Underwood and Guscott had minor chances during the first half. However, this more expansive approach inevitably meant that the Australians were afforded opportunities of their own and it was from one of these that Australia managed the game's only try. A Campese kick set Tim Horan free to earn a line-out a few yards from England's line. Ofahengaue caught and then fed the ball to Tony Daly, who touched down with the help of McKenzie.

The situation looked bleak for England, and they trailed Australia 0-9 at the interval. But Richard Hill, Paul Ackford and Mike Teague had let it be known that this would be their final game for England, and such seasoned veterans were not about to bring the curtain down on their careers with a whimper. Collectively the side resolved that if they were to go down, they would do so fighting.

A fierce 40 minutes followed, with England enjoying the lion's share of possession and demonstrating considerable attacking prowess. Two Jonathan Webb penalties were their reward. One from a Campese knock-on that Brian Moore later suggested would have resulted in a try for Underwood. Six points was a respectable haul but it was not enough and the resolute Australian defence held on for a deserved 6-12 victory.

So the World Cup went to Australia, and Twickenham Stadium echoed to sounds of Waltzing Matilda as the Queen presented the trophy to Nick Farr-Jones, the Australian captain who had been at the heart of the Wallabies second-half defence.

Australia had got the job done. Over the course of the tournament they had played the best rugby, and were worthy recipients of the Webb Ellis Cup. Of the English players who dejectedly left Twickenham that day, only Jason Leonard would one day get the opportunity to reverse his disappointment.

Aftermath

When the dust settled, the 1991 Rugby World Cup had been an enormous success in every respect. It inspired a new generation of rugby participants all over the globe. Events at Twickenham had been beamed into the homes of millions of television viewers around the world. Crucially, it had also been an overwhelming commercial success, generating an estimated £20 million for the IRB.

More controversially, the revenues unlocked by the World Cup instigated an age-old and very public debate about who should benefit from them. Rob Andrew, on the day of the World Cup Final, made his opinions known, predicting that 'change' was inevitable.

28

A Professional Stadium for a Professional Game

When architect Terry Ward was approached by the RFU, in 1988, his instructions were clear – Twickenham Stadium was to be nothing less than the finest sports stadium in the world. But the transformation wouldn't happen overnight, the new stadium would be built in four stages over a number of years, starting with Archibald Leitch's old North Stand, built in 1924.

The North Stand would be ready to host the Rugby World Cup in 1991. Implicit in its design was the notion that it be replicated around the ground in a continuous 'wrap-around' style. The stand would be the first fully three-tiered stand in Britain. Initially, the plan was for the bottom tier to be terracing for standing fans. Had this design been pursued the completed stadium would have had a capacity of 125,000.

The 1991 Rugby World Cup represented the meridian point between the old and the new for Twickenham Stadium. The scale and ambition of the future was embodied in the North Stand, looming large over the rest of the ground. Opposite, stood the unloved 1981 South Stand and between them the treasured, iconic extended East and West Stands that had remained mostly unaltered since Bernard Gadney had made his full test debut back in 1932.

North, East, West, South

Following the same pattern of development as the 1920s, the East Stand was next. Ward shocked the committee in the development stages for the East Stand by informing them that the replacement would need to be over 100 feet in height. Unperturbed RFU Grounds Committee Chairman Tony Hallett, who emerged internally as the RFU's driving force for the on-going project, replied, 'we're big men, we're doing a big job. Let's go for it.'

As soon as the Rugby World Cup had finished, the developers moved in. Two years later, the structure and inner seating were complete and attention was turned to the interior fit-out of the space underneath the seating bowl. A large restaurant, initially called 'Invincibles', in homage to Cyril Brownlie's touring New Zealand side of 1924/25, was furnished, alongside the Young England Rugby Bar that served alcohol free drinks and the stadium's first purpose-built museum.

Hidden Treasure

Since 1871, the RFU had been steadily acquiring relics and, in 1996, the 'Museum of Rugby', rebranded in 2007 as the 'World Rugby Museum', would henceforward be given the responsibility of caring for them. It also provided a semi-permanent home for rugby's oldest trophy. The Calcutta Cup had come into existence in 1878. The disbanded Calcutta Football Club had emptied her coffers of 270 silver rupees, which were melted down and crafted into a beautifully ornate patterned silver tankard with cobra snake-handles and a small viceroy elephant on top of the lid. The trophy has been declared for the winner of England v. Scotland ever since and, provided England are the winners, it remains on permanent display in the World Rugby Museum until the sides meet again.

Inside the West

Work began on the West Stand in 1994 and the inner bowl was completed later that year. Work continued underneath and inside of the stand well into 1995, where the facilities of the older stand were replaced and enhanced. Although functional and grey on the outside, the inside was to be a vision of corporate modernity. The new stand would include four dressing rooms, including the home and away dressing rooms, which lay either side of the player's tunnel. Behind them, facing the West Concourse, a glass-fronted entrance with stairs and a lift leading up to the Spirit of Rugby restaurant. On top of that were the committee rooms, including an oak-panelled council room, spacious members' lounge and the RFU president's suite. In between and around the central staircase, memorable items from the older stand were reinstated. Included were the collection of centenary gifts, presented to the RFU by their national equivalents around the world in 1971; a Springbok head, which had hung inside the West Stand since London Counties defeated South Africa at Twickenham in 1951; and William Barnes Wollen's famous 'Roses Match' painting, depicting the county final of 1893, that hung on the wall of the president's room.

With three sides now complete, the stadium had a variety of additional rooms such as the stewards' room, the dining cellar, the East Stand rugby store, and a large room tucked away on the ground floor of the West Stand called the ERIC room. ERIC stands for 'England Rugby Internationals Club' and is a function room reserved solely for those who have worn the red rose of England. The ERIC room had begun life, as the Internationals Bar in 1947, as a simple hut in which the players could get a drink after the game. It was put to good use and Chris Winn later recalled seeing the likes of Richard Burton and Elizabeth Taylor mixing with the players after the England v. Wales game in 1954. In 1995, it found its way into the permanent fabric of the stadium, under the West Stand.

In addition were 155 corporate boxes. To service these were thirty-two kitchens. As the game turned professional, corporate hospitality would quickly establish itself as one the RFU's single biggest revenue drivers, the stadium benefitting, in a way that could not have been envisaged in 1907, by its close proximity to Heathrow Airport.

Guardians of the Gate

With the West Stand done, the RFU felt that the development required a splash of culture to complete it. That responsibility fell to Tony Hallett, by now RFU chief executive, who put an ad in the newspaper. Farquhar Laing, son of pop artist and sculptor Gerald Laing, answered the call, and the father and son team set to work. In 1994, four bronze figures were unveiled on top of the Rowland Hill Memorial Gates, which had been repositioned as a gateway through which the players would pass on matchdays into the West Stand and the player's tunnel. In the middle of the gate, in between the four players, stood a coade stone lion that had been given to the RFU by the Greater London Council in 1970, and likely derived from the Lion Brewery that once towered over Waterloo Bridge. The lion was given a gilded gold coat and turned to face our foes in the west.

And so the stadium was complete. Or was it? Until relatively recently, the South Stand had been the highest point in the stadium, but was now dwarfed by the roof teeth of the East and West Stands, jutting out high above the south try line. The RFU had something even grander in mind for the South, but before plans could be drawn up they would have to address a familiar problem.

Another trip to the local estate agent was in order.

The Men Who Made Twickenham: No. 4 – Terry Ward

The awarding of the Rugby World Cup focused minds within the RFU and, in 1988, they took consultation regarding the redevelopment of the stadium. The instructions were to increase ground capacity by rebuilding the North Stand in a way that would facilitate future redevelopment to both the East and West Stands.

Husband & Co. were awarded the contract and Terry Ward was the chief architect. Ward knew his rugby and paid a visit to Parc des Princes in Paris, a ground that allowed spectators to get up close to the action. In order to keep fans close to the playing surface, it was decided that a three-tier stand was required, and Twickenham's North Stand became the first fully three-tiered stand in Great Britain.

Work began on the East and West Stands soon after, as Twickenham Stadium continued its transformation into a twenty-first-century stadium. Ward was the architect not just for the stadium build but also the intricate fit-outs inside the West Stand that included the dressing rooms, Spirit of Rugby restaurant, committee rooms and national fitness centre.

Ward's stated intention was to 'create a stadium for England that would give them a five point advantage in every home game they played'.

When the time came to begin the redevelopment of the South Stand, the RFU turned to Terry Ward once more. Now of Ward McHugh Associates, Ward set about designing one of the most intricate stands in sport. The South Stand not only completed the three-tiered, wrap-around interior seating, but included a 156-room hotel, conference, banqueting and office space, theatre, retail store and underground swimming pool.

The Men Who Made Twickenham: No. 5 – Alf Wright

The family of Alfred Robert Frederick Wright moved to Twickenham the same year that the old ground opened in 1909. As a young man,

Alf took up employment as a clerk with the RFU in 1920. He would remain as an employee, and later archivist, for more than sixty years. He is credited with having standardised the design of the England rose, which, up until 1920, the players themselves had supplied in a variety of shapes and sizes. During the Second World War, Alf was called up by the War Office, but when hostilities ceased he returned to Twickenham to continue his valuable work.

For most of his lengthy tenure, Alf resided in No. 180 Whitton Road and took it upon himself to collect and preserve the ever growing collection of books, photographs and relics that the RFU had been amassing since 1871.

In this way, Alf paved the groundwork for the collection upon which the World Rugby Museum would eventually be built. Like many others, Alf was convinced that the 1981 South Stand development was a mistake and took particular umbrage at the assertion that the South Terrace was unsafe for spectators. Unsurprisingly, over the years, he had formed a deep emotional bond with the stadium as it was during its classic phase, and saw no reason that such perfection need ever be changed. He recalled the days when players, ex-players and fans alike would share a beer and a story under the clock tower on the South Terrace, a place that he believed encapsulated all that was wonderful in the spirit of rugby.

He therefore took great pleasure when the demolition men wasted two weeks in a variety of futile efforts to deconstruct the famous old terrace. 'Unsafe indeed,' he muttered in admiration of workmanship that he himself had borne witness.

Though he could accept that the South Stand development was ultimately necessary, the old West and East Stand were, for him, sacrosanct. He believed, their concave line-hugging design, with each seat affixed to a steel rivet, would last 1,000 years and when they were eventually replaced it would have been a moment of great sadness and loss for Alf Wright.

The rate of change may explain why, when officials visited him to see what material they might install in the new museum, they discovered 'little of interest'. But today, the RFU Archive inside the World Rugby Museum is filled to the brim with relics and books, many presented to the RFU and signed by such luminaries as George Rowland Hill, Adrian Stoop, William Wavell Wakefield and Bill Ramsey, each of them a tribute to the meticulous care shown to them by Alfred Wright. Here lies his legacy to a game and a place that he loved.

West Stand demolition.

Left: Calcutta Cup, 1879.

Above: Corporate box, 2011.

Above right: Inside the England dressing room, 2009.

Above far right: North Stand opening, 1991.

Below far right: Players' tunnel.

Below right: East Stand, 1992.

Above: The baths since 1931.

Above right: East Stand.

Right: The view from the North Stand, *c.* 1996.

Left: Twickenham Stadium, late 1990s.

Above: West Stand council room.

Left: The Lion, 1971.

Allez les Blues

Wales were the proud hosts of the 1999 Rugby World Cup and, like England in 1991, they chose to share key matches with their neighbours. This meant that Twickenham would be called upon to host all of England's pool matches and both semi-finals.

The chance of a home semi-final was lost when a record five dropped goals from South Africa's Jannie de Beer ended England's campaign at the quarter-final stage. Not to be deterred, thousands of English rugby fans bought tickets for the semi-finals regardless, and for those that purchased tickets for the second contest between New Zealand and France, a treat was in store.

The Most Spectacular Comeback in World Cup History

New Zealand had once again started as pre-tournament favourites, with the likes of Tana Umaga and Jonah Lomu at the peak of their powers. The All Blacks started strongly, with two first-half tries from Lomu setting up a 24-10 half-time lead. Presumably in a deep malaise,

most of the French team were spotted smoking cigarettes by a member of the Twickenham ground staff during the interval. Whether this tale is true or not is uncertain, but what is beyond question is that, in the second half, France were rejuvenated.

Fly-half Christophe Lamaison added to his first-half try by kicking two dropped goals and two penalties, and all of a sudden France were back in touch. The excited, mostly English, Twickenham crowd then threw their weight behind the French team, and an unusual symbiosis occurred. France, who would never have experienced such overwhelming support inside Twickenham Stadium before, were inspired. Three tries in quick succession floored New Zealand, propelling the French out of sight and on the road to a 43-31 victory. Les Bleus were in the final, and thousands of English voices joined the French in singing *La Marseillaise* for the first and very probably last time in the stadium's history.

Cardiff would host the final and England's involvement was long since ended, but Twickenham Stadium had hosted the most spectacular comeback in World Cup history.

7s Series

The World 7s Series began in the 1999/2000 season and comprised ten tournaments, including the Hong Kong 7s, which began in 1976. Points were awarded in the order that national teams finished after a knock-out contest in each round and then aggregated over the ten rounds to establish a series winner.

At the start of the 2000/01 season, it was announced that Twickenham would be added to the roster as the venue for the series showpiece. Since then, the London 7s has steadily grown in popularity, becoming an established May feature in the stadium's annual events calendar.

Having a Ball

7s rugby has always been associated with fun, both on and off the pitch, and it may be for this reason that university students have made the London 7s their own. If you happen to find yourself in Twickenham town centre on the Saturday morning of the 7s, don't be at all surprised to find yourself surrounded by monkeys, bumblebees, African dictators, cowgirls or spacemen. Each year is now given a fancy-dress theme that has included '70s disco, beach party and safari.

By 2010, the event was attracting up to 80,000 visitors over the two days. This has since increased to almost 110,000, making the London

7s officially the most popular event on the Twickenham calendar. Though England have never managed to win the series, Twickenham has proved lucky for the home side on several occasions, notably 2003, 2004 and 2009.

Spectators getting into the spirit of 7s rugby.

All Conquerors

For all of the talented XVs that England had selected since the opening of Twickenham Stadium, none could honestly claim to have mastered the challenge of the southern hemisphere. Will Carling, Bill Beaumont, John Pullin and Bernard Gadney all had their moments. But these rare instances of triumph merely stemmed the tide of southern domination. It would take a truly special side change the natural order.

Clive Woodward was appointed England coach when Jack Rowell retired at the end of the 1996/97 season. His reign started brightly with home draws against Australia and New Zealand, followed by a creditable second place in the 1998 Five Nations Championship.

The side he had inherited was a mixture of well-established names, such as Martin Johnson, Jason Leonard and Jeremy Guscott; along with a number of impressive emerging talents, ready to stake their claims for inclusion.

Rowell and Carling had led England to the semi-finals of the 1995 World Cup in South Africa, only to be steamrollered by the irrepressible physicality of New Zealand's Jonah Lomu. Lomu was a new breed of rugby player, and if England were going to compete in the professional age, they would need to find players that could match him for strength.

New Kids on the Block

Wasps' Lawrence Dallaglio was exactly that kind of player. He made his debut for England in 1995 and, for the next three seasons, was shifted around the back row before Woodward installed him at No. 8, from where he would earn the majority of his eighty-five caps. Impressed by his all-action brand of rugby, Woodward also made him his captain.

In 1998, a nineteen-year-old fly-half from Newcastle Falcons was added to the mix. Jonny Wilkinson, although raw, had game awareness beyond his years and had helped his club side to their first Premiership title earlier that year. His first start for England, however, was a catastrophe and England sunk to their largest ever defeat, 0-76 against Australia in Brisbane. It was the lowest point on what would come to be known as the 'tour from hell'. Few would have predicted in its aftermath that Wilkinson would go on to become the most famous rugby player that England has ever produced.

The following year, England came within a whisker of a Grand Slam, but a last-minute converted try for Wales at Wembley condemned England to a 31-32 defeat, ensuring Scotland would end the millennium as champions. Despite this setback, Clive Woodward went into the 1999 Rugby World Cup with high hopes for his developing side. But, as in previous tournaments, southern hemisphere sides stood in their way.

Pieces of the Puzzle

New Zealand beat England comfortably in the group stages and subsequent injuries to key players left Woodward's side with little chance against South Africa in the quarter-final. They lost 22-44, Jannie De Beer setting a new record with five dropped goals.

Woodward was roundly criticised for the exit and calls for his head were made in the aftermath of the tournament. The RFU, however, stood by their man, believing, as he claimed, that the jigsaw puzzle that was the England XV was starting to come together.

A back row trio of Neil Back, Lawrence Dallaglio and Richard Hill had become established, and was beginning to develop into one of the most combative and feared units England had ever fielded. Their mastery of the breakdown was starting to exert considerable control over games, resulting in possession or penalties, either of which Jonny Wilkinson could capitalise upon.

Wilkinson himself, though still a rookie, was developing into one of the world's most complete players, his athleticism and skill able to cut open defences, while his metronomic kicking of penalties and conversions ensured that the scoreboard was never idle for long. His partnership with Matt Dawson would become the best England half-back partnership since Davies and Kershaw.

Amid the front five, there was much competition for places and frequent changes, invariably with only one exception. Martin Johnson had matured into one of the most commanding leaders England had ever produced. Woodward would place a premium on his side remaining calm under pressure, and in Johnson he had the perfect exponent. Although the coach would later comment that he had leaders all over the pitch, Johnson was without question his commander in the field.

Setting Down a Marker

Further evidence that this was an improving side arrived the following year when England claimed the first Six Nations Championship, despite a final round defeat to Scotland in Edinburgh. After the defeat to South Africa, Woodward had claimed that they would have won the game had all of their players been available, and, later in 2000, he would get the opportunity to prove it. A tied series in South Africa set up a decider at Twickenham during the autumn internationals, but before that an even bigger challenge awaited in the form of world champions Australia.

A packed 74,000 sell-out crowd watched as Woodward's side finally clicked. Australia were ahead 15-19 as the game entered injury time, but the Twickenham faithful were sent into delirium when winger Dan Luger chased down an Iain Balshaw chip to score in the corner. With no time remaining on the clock, Wilkinson delivered the coup de grâce by kicking the conversion to give England a 22-19 victory. It was the first time that England had won the Cook Cup, and would be the first of five straight victories against the Wallabies.

After beating the world champions, South Africa didn't seem like quite so daunting a challenge, and England duly dispatched the Springboks a fortnight later with a hard fought 25-17 victory.

Grand Slam Certainties?

England went into the 2001 Six Nations in imperious form. Victories over the southern hemisphere opposition had given them a self-confidence that allowed them to not only beat sides but to completely dominate them. Twickenham watched, as England defeated Scotland by 43-3 and France 48-19. A first Grand Slam since 1995 seemed all but certain, until events outside of rugby put the brakes on.

An outbreak of the foot-and-mouth disease meant that England's final game in Dublin was cancelled until October. Inevitably England lost the rescheduled fixture and had to settle for a championship victory but no Grand Slam. Despite this, England were in good shape and were even threatening to improve.

The exodus of talented rugby players that came in the wake of the 1895 split had only come to an end in 1995, when Rugby Union finally became a professional sport. Since then, slowly but surely, the trend had begun to reverse, and was now about to impact on the national setup in spectacular fashion.

Billy Whizz

Jason Robinson had won every Rugby League domestic honour with club side Wigan Warriors and had even appeared in a Rugby League World Cup final in 1995, before switching codes in 2000. His free-spirited attacking style and safe hands made an immediate impact with Sale Sharks, and he made his first start for England the following year.

The autumn offered England the opportunity to prove that last year's victories against Australia and South Africa had not been one offs. For the opening game against the Wallabies, Robinson was switched to full-back with a license to roam. England won 21-15. In the following game, Robinson ran in four tries in a 134-0 victory against Romania – Twickenham and England's largest ever. That just left South Africa and for the third game in a row, England marked their dominance over the Springboks, this time winning 29-9.

Sergeant Wilko

In 2002, for the seventh year running, England missed out on a Grand Slam by a single game. This time it was France's turn to stop them, but England still put in some memorable performances, most notably against Ireland at Twickenham.

Ireland themselves were a fast improving side, but came up against an England player who was about to announce himself as one of the very best in world rugby.

This was Jonny Wilkinson's finest performance in an England jersey. He kicked fifteen points, but it was his incisive running and quick hands that most impressed, making a try for Ben Cohen and scoring one himself. In the end England won 45-11. It was their fourteenth straight victory at Twickenham, a new record and it earned the stadium a new nickname – 'Fortress Twickenham'.

Having racked up back-to-back wins against Australia and South Africa, England now had only one side in their sights. They had not beaten the All Blacks since the days of Will Carling back in 1993, but the class of 2002 had no reason to fear anyone.

The game was a classic. Wilkinson kicked the early penalties before Jonah Lomu grabbed a try for New Zealand. England countered with a try from Robinson and then another by Lewis Moody, to lead 17-14 at the break. Wilkinson, who had already scored one drop-kick in the first half, looked set for another before instead opting to chip over the New Zealand backline and sprint through to touch down for a sublime try that had the entire Twickenham crowd on its feet. A converted try from Cohen gave England a 31-14 lead, before New Zealand hit back. The visitors doubled their tally in the final 20 minutes and came close to winning, but England held on for a 31-28 victory. Was the south tamed at last?

Their next game against Australia was equally thrilling. This time it was England that had to come back from 16-28 down in the second half. They did so to claim a 32-31 victory, their third over the world champions in as many years. In their third and final autumn international, England smashed the Springboks by 53-3, their largest ever victory against South Africa.

Number One

For English rugby fans, this was the stuff that dreams are made of. England had scored consecutive victories over all three southern hemisphere giants, the first and only time such a feat has ever been achieved. That they had achieved dominance over the southern giants was confirmed at the end of 2002 when the Zurich World Rugby Rankings were published and for the first time ever England were on top.

However, there remained lingering concerns as England entered 2003, World Cup year. For seven years running England had missed out on a Grand Slam by a single victory. Was this evidence that the side would choke when it came to the big prizes? The Six Nations offered England the chance to prove otherwise.

They began the campaign with arguably their toughest fixture. France were the reigning champions, but England had home advantage. Wilkinson's boot gave England the lead at half-time, before a Robinson try produced a comfortable gap. France came back with a late flourish and two tries but England held on for a 25-17 win. Wins against Wales, Italy and Scotland followed setting up a championship decider against Ireland in Dublin. This time, unlike in 2001, there was no foot-and-mouth outbreak to slow the England juggernaut and Martin Johnson's men steamrollered their way to a 42-6 victory.

After a run of seven near misses, England had at last secured the Grand Slam, and their third Championship success in four seasons. And just to rubber stamp their mastery of the southern hemisphere, they completed back-to-back away wins over New Zealand and Australia in Wellington and Melbourne in the summer of 2003. They would take the Six Nations Championship, the Triple Crown and successive away victories against New Zealand and Australia into their World Cup campaign.

All Conquerors

Having reached the top of the international pecking order, the world cup was all about maintaining their balance. Woodward's side weathered strong challenges from Samoa and South Africa to top their group, before a thrilling quarter-final with Wales. The Welsh had the better of the first half and led 10-3 shortly after half-time, before Robinson evaded five tackles to score a try that helped bring England level. It would be England's only try, the rest of their points coming by way of Wilkinson's boot for a 28-17 victory.

A controlled 24-7 victory over France saw England into the final where they would face the hosts, Australia in Sydney. Another outstanding try from Robinson saw England take a 14-5 lead, but second-half profligacy and repeated punishment for scrum engagement allowed Australia to claw the scores back to 14-14, taking the game into extra time. With both sides tiring, the Wallabies began to fancy their chances but instead their efforts only enabled the fairytale ending. With seconds remaining, Johnson and Dawson zig-zagged their talismanic fly-half into position. All that remained was for Jonny Wilkinson to calmly drop-kick his side to a 20-17 victory. The Webb Ellis Cup was coming home.

England's victory in the 2003 Rugby World Cup would be English rugby's finest hour. For all the achievements of Poulton, Wakefield, Evans,

Beaumont and Carling, none had achieved mastery over all of their rivals in the way that Martin Johnson's side had. The victory in Sydney was the crowning achievement, securing England's place in the history books as the first northern hemisphere side to win the Rugby World Cup.

List of Victories

Date	Opposition	Town/City	Score
23/03/2002	Wales	London	50-10
6/04/2002	Italy	Rome	45-9
22/06/2002	Argentina	Buenos Aires	26-18
9/09/2002	New Zealand	London	31-28
16/09/2002	Australia	London	32-31
23/11/2002	South Africa	London	53-3
15/02/2003	France	London	25-17
22/02/2003	Wales	Cardiff	26-9
9/03/2003	Italy	London	40-5
22/03/2003	Scotland	London	40-9
30/03/2003	Ireland	Dublin	42-6
14/06/2003	New Zealand	Wellington	15-13
21/06/2003	Australia	Melbourne	25-14
23/08/2003	Wales	Cardiff	43-9
6/09/2003	France	London	45-14
12/10/2003	Georgia	Perth	84-6
18/10/2003	South Africa	Perth	25-6
26/10/2003	Samoa	Melbourne	35-22
2/11/2003	Uruguay	Brisbane	111-13
9/09/2003	Wales	Brisbane	28-17
16/09/2003	France	Sydney	24-7
22/11/2003	Australia	Sydney	20-17

England supporter Peter Cross, 2006.

England fans, 2003.

Italy fans.

32

24-Hour Twickenham

By the time planning permission was sought for the South Stand development, the RFU owned no fewer than twelve houses on Whitton Road. A further two remained in places that would pose an obstruction to the development and these were duly purchased.

The early years of professionalism had been good to the RFU and the improved stadium had generated funds that allowed the RFU to integrate locally in a way that had not previously been possible. As with earlier attempts to alter the fabric of the South Stand, local residents' opinion would be crucial to the planning application. Earmarked within the proposal were £1.4 million of investment into local town centre improvements as well as a broader commitment to local arts projects.

The Largest Rugby Stadium in the World

Planning permission was duly granted in 2004 for an £80-million South Stand that would increase the capacity of the stadium from 75,000 to 82,000, making Twickenham Stadium the largest stadium in the world devoted solely to the sport of rugby.

But that wasn't all. The RFU had secured a number of commercial partners and the South Stand would include: a Virgin Active health-club with a 50-metre swimming pool, a 156-room four-star Marriot hotel, a theatre, a new rugby store and a new 'Rugby House' – office space that would house 205 of the RFU's full-time workforce. The vision was for Twickenham Stadium to become a 365-day-a-year, round-the-clock destination for visitors and engine room of the local economy.

Before work could begin, there was a small matter of demolishing the existing South Stand, and fourteen Edwardian villas on the south side of Whitton Road. But once this was complete the space would allow for a considerably enlarged footprint, which would include a broad pedestrianized promenade south of the South Stand, where Whitton Road met Rugby Road.

The inner bowl was reopened in time for the November internationals of 2006 and a record 82,076 people were present to witness the *new* new South Stand make its Test debut during the England New Zealand tie. Meanwhile, work continued on the outside, which resembled a building site until 2008.

The 24/7 Twickenham Experience

The following year, the Marriot Hotel opened for business with a surprise up its sleeve. Tucked in between the second and third tiers of the South Stand, are a line of curtained windows. These six hotel suites, overlooking the pitch, were instantly instated as the most expensive seats in the house, allowing those who could afford it a match-day like no other.

With work complete and Terry Ward's vision now fully realised, Twickenham stood proud as the largest, most modern rugby stadium in the world. On any given non-matchday the site remains a hive of activity, with visitors from all over the world checking into the hotel and restaurant, before passing through Heathrow airport, local residents making early morning and evening visits to the health club, rugby fans from all over the world visiting the World Rugby Museum and winding their way around the stadium as part of a Twickenham Stadium Tour before spending their hard-earned money in the rugby store. On top of all that, the stadium is home to around 300 full-time employees, mostly based in the Rugby House office complex in the South Stand.

Rugby Houses

Rugby House had begun life as a dilapidated old Georgian Villa on the end of Whitton Road, before being transferred to one the Edwardian houses further along the same road. It had then found its spiritual home as the 'office' inside the classic West Stand, where it remained until the permanent staff complement increased up to a point that a new office solution was required. In 1977, the Prince of Wales formally opened the new Rugby House in the south-east corner of the stadium concourse. Then, when the South Stand development began, the RFU became tenants in a purpose-built office building facing the stadium from the other side of Rugby Road, before moving into the South Stand permanently when the stadium was complete.

Although the stadium prides itself on being the largest rugby stadium in the world, preparations were also made for night-time activity of a quite different variety. The thought of 60,000 rock fans standing somewhere above his perfectly manicured pitch was probably not overly-appealing to head groundsman Keith Kent, so it probably helped that the first act to perform at the stadium was his favourite band. In 2003, The Rolling Stones became the first of a number of major music acts to perform at the stadium.

Meet Me at the Line-Out

Midway through 2009, RFU chief executive Francis Baron found himself in a similar position to his predecessor, Tony Hallet, back in 1994. With the structural development complete, a final artistic flourish was required and, like Tony, Francis determined that a public sculpture would be appropriate. Once again the Laing family pitched their concept and Gerald, now in his seventies, was awarded the commission, along with his son's foundry Black Isle Bronze.

The magnificent Core Values statue was unveiled on the site of the old Rugby House in 2010, during Twickenham Stadium's centenary season. It had taken 100 years, but Cail's folly and William's Cabbage Patch were complete at last.

Above: England fans, 2009.

Right: Core values sculpture, 2010.

Left: Aerial image of stadium.

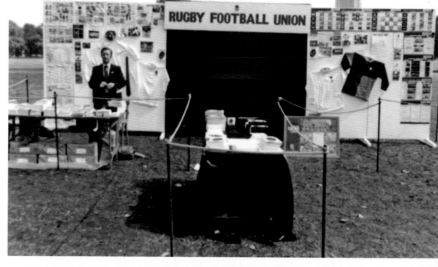

Above: South Stand demolition, 2005.

Above right: Rugby retail, 1971.

Right: South Stand exterior.

Left: Opening of South Stand interior, 2006.

Architect plans, 2009.

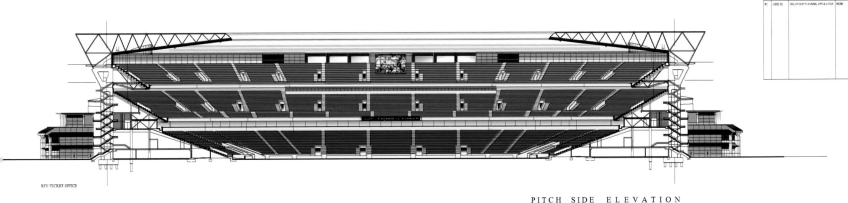

RFU TICKET OFFICE

PITCH SIDE ELEVATION

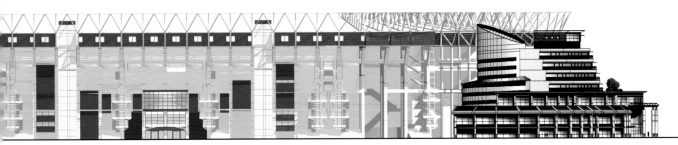

RFU STORE

WEST ELEVATION

RUGBY FOOTBALL UNION

REDEVELOPMENT OF THE
SOUTH STAND

TWICKENHAM

DRAWING TITLE
NORTH AND WEST ELEVATIONS

WARD
McHUGH
ASSOCIATES

ARUP

SCALE
1:500

PROJECT NO.	DRAWING NO.	REV
7087	A/L/017	F

33

Twickenham's Centenary

In 100 years, the stadium that William Cail had built back in 1909 had changed beyond recognition. Gone were the South Terrace and the single-decked East and West Stands, gone even were their replacements and Archibald Leitch's old North Stand. In their place stood Terry Ward's masterpiece, the largest rugby stadium in the world and one of the world's most prestigious sports and entertainment venues.

To mark the stadium's centenary, a number of events were planned, foremost among which was the Six Nations visit of Wales. Wales had been the first visiting international side to visit Twickenham back in 1910 and the fixture calendar dictated that they would be the first of the stadium's second century. Victory against Wales had kick-started an unprecedented period of success for Adrian Stoop's England, and there was significant pressure on the 2010 side to do likewise.

To mark the occasion, shirt sponsors Nike had produced a retro design kit that took its inspiration from the jerseys that Stoop's side would have worn. Cream coloured, it would include a button-up collar and would not feature a shirt-sponsor.

The Centenary Match

Wales had won Grand Slams in 2005 and 2008, but England, coached by Martin Johnson, were an improving side and, unlike in 1909 where Wales were overwhelming favourites, the two sides went into the contest on an equal footing.

Appropriately, it was Jonny Wilkinson who kicked off the second century and landed the first points with a penalty. Tries either side of half-time, including a brilliant solo effort from Danny Care, gave England a 20-3 lead, before Wales responded with two tries of their own to move within three points at 20-17. With the game now on a knife-edge, an interception and quick hands between Toby Flood and Matthew Tait led to a match-winning try, giving England a 30-17 victory.

The Greatest Ever

Since 2005, the World Rugby Museum had been honouring the greatest performers whose careers had come to an end, by installing them on their wall of fame and erecting blue plaques around the stadium. These players comprised the shortlist for an internet poll to determine Twickenham's Player of the Century. At the same time, another poll was created to determine Twickenham's Try of the Century.

An invitation-only gala dinner was arranged in the South Stand's largest function room, the Rose Room, where unsurprisingly

England's world-cup-winning captain and incumbent coach Martin Johnson received the Player of the Century award. Modest by nature, Johnson attributed the victory to his association with the all-conquering side of 2003.

Perhaps more surprisingly, but no less deservingly, the Try of the Century award went to Frenchman Philippe Saint-Andre, whose try in 1991 had so nearly cost Will Carling's side its first Grand Slam. The try itself was initiated by Serge Blanco, from behind the French try line, and few would argue that it is one of the greatest of all time.

Player of the Century Poll

Name	Total	%
Martin Johnson (England)	3262	10.5
Gareth Edwards (Wales)	2325	7.5
Jason Robinson (England)	1996	6.4
Lawrence Dallaglio (England)	1826	5.9
Richard Hill (England)	1807	5.8
Jonah Lomu (New Zealand)	1799	5.8
David Duckham (England)	1661	5.3
Rory Underwood (England)	1652	5.3
Neil Back (England)	1649	5.3
Serge Blanco (France)	1635	5.3

RIght: England *v.* Wales, 2010.

Far right: Matin Johnson receives Player of the Century award, 2009.

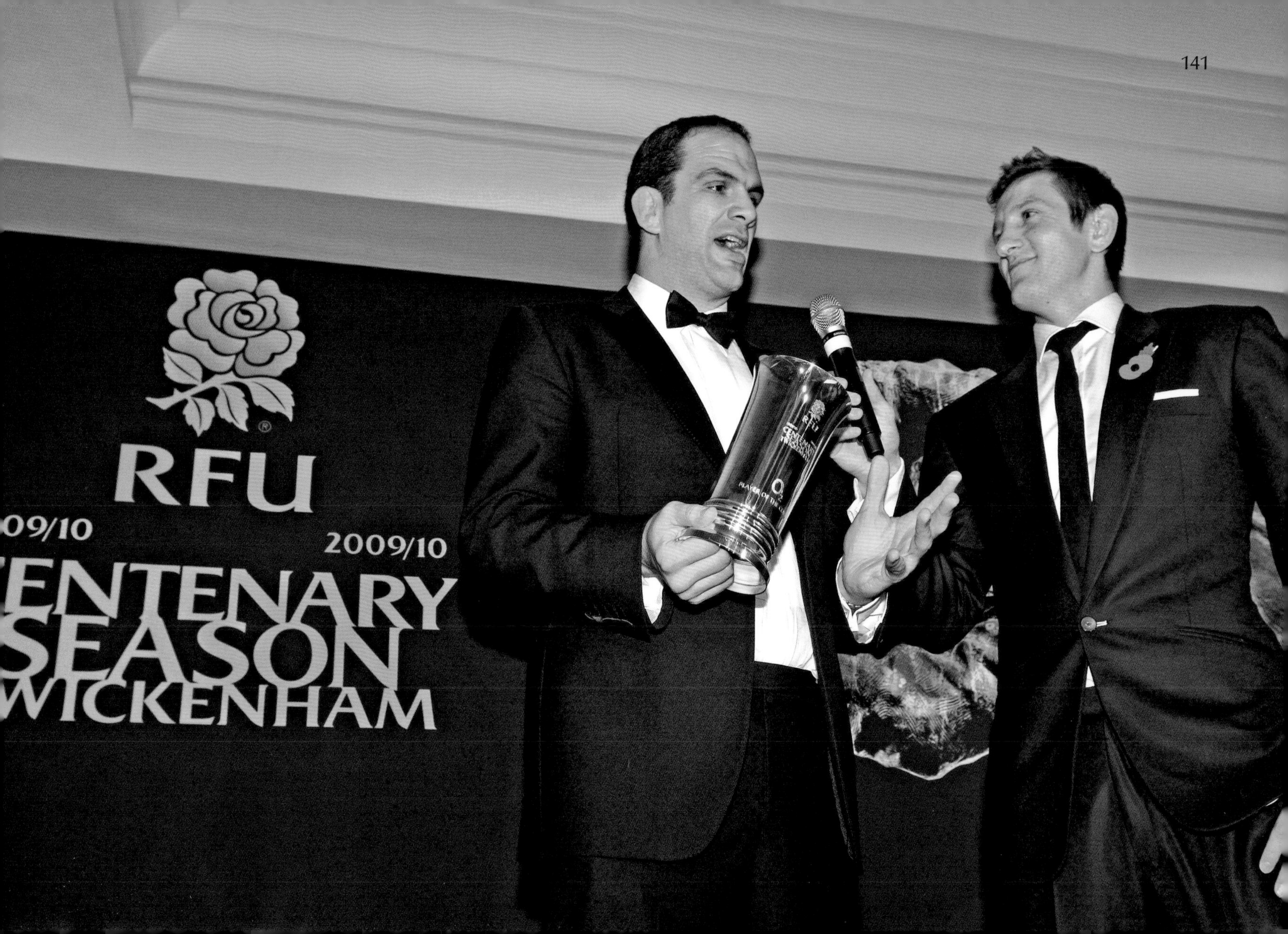
RFU
2009/10

Above: England *v.* Wales, 2010.

Above left: Centenary ambassadors outside the West Stand, 2009.

Left: World Rugby Museum Wall of Fame, 2013.

Right: Twickenham Stadium's centenary season, 2009.

Steve Borthwick, England *v.* Wales, 2010.

34

A Nation Awaits

In the months after securing the Webb Ellis Cup, Martin Johnson and several other key players announced their retirements, and so it was no surprise that England entered another period of rebuilding.

Brian Ashton was appointed England coach at the end of 2006, helping England to their largest-ever victory against Wales – 62-5, in a warm-up encounter for the 2007 World Cup. Against the odds, his side defeated Australia and France to reach the final of the tournament, where they were narrowly defeated by South Africa.

Ashton took his side to second place in the 2008 Six Nations Championship, before former captain Martin Johnson was unveiled as the next England coach. Johnson's side retained several key players from the side that he had led to victory in Sydney such as Jonny Wilkinson, Mike Tindall and Phil Vickery. The side also contained a sprinkling of top-class performers who had established themselves since – among them Sale's Andrew Sheridan, who had announced his status as one of the world's most effective loosehead props, with his demolition job on Australia and, in particular, Guy Shepherdson during the 2007 World Cup.

The Makings of a New Side

Johnson repeated Ashton's trick by taking second place in 2009, before an inconsistent 2010 season forced changes. Northampton Saints' Ben Foden was selected at full-back, and his clubmate Chris Ashton, who had gained a reputation as a prolific tryscorer since his switch from Rugby League was selected on the wing. Lewis 'Mad Dog' Moody, Leicester Tiger's long-serving flanker, was instated as captain.

The new side clicked against Australia in the autumn. Toby Flood kicked a record twenty-five points, while Chris Ashton scored two tries, the second of which was an all-time Twickenham classic. It began when Tindall succeeded in a turnover on the England try line. The ball was then quickly distributed to Ashton on the wing, who ran almost 90 metres before touching down with a trademark swallow dive.

England took their good form into the 2011 Six Nations Championship, winning 26-19 in Cardiff, thanks to two tries from Ashton and a match-winning performance from fly-half Toby Flood. Ashton added four more tries against Italy, and England then won a bruising arm-wrestle of a contest at home against the reigning champions France. A home win against the Scots all but guaranteed the championship, setting up a Grand Slam decider against Ireland in Dublin. This proved to be a bridge too far for the developing side, as Brian O'Driscoll inspired the home side to a 24-8 victory. The championship win was followed by a disappointing 2011 World Cup and Johnson stepped down as coach.

Setting Down a Marker

Stuart Lancaster then began rebuilding the side, making Harlequins' flanker Chris Robshaw his captain at the start of 2012. Other debutantes included nineteen-year-old Owen Farrell, a nerveless young Saracens player, whose father Andy had represented England and was now part of Lancaster's back-room staff. The new look side took a respectable second place in the Six Nations Championship, before coming of age with a magnificent autumn victory against world champions New Zealand.

New Zealand were at the end of a twenty game unbeaten run, a period that included their long-awaited world cup triumph in Auckland. Most pre-match speculation concerned how many points England might lose by. England, however, had different ideas. Farrell showed ice-cold composure by kicking England into a 15-0 lead just after half-time. New Zealand then struck back with two converted tries, which left most England supporters fearing the worse. But Lancaster's England seemed possessed of a steelier resilience than before and began to put on a show.

Leicester Tiger's Manu Tuilagi, who had been among the England set up for little over a year, set out his credentials as an international wrecking-ball. His unstoppable forays from outside-centre wrought havoc in the All Blacks' defence. He, Ashton and Brad Barritt all scored tries as England stretched out a twenty-point lead. The final score was 38-21, England's largest-ever win over the All Blacks.

Dragon's Lair

This gave the side momentum going into the 2013 Six Nations Championship, and wins against Scotland, Ireland France and Italy were duly secured, leaving only Wales at the Millennium Stadium in Cardiff between Lancaster's side and a Grand Slam. Wales were the reigning champions but had lost their opening game of the series against Ireland. Since then they had gone from strength to strength and knew that a victory by more than 6 points would allow them to retain their title.

Home advantage was crucial, and for England's relatively inexperienced side, eleven of whom had never played in Cardiff before, the occasion was too much. Without ever getting a foothold in the game they lost 3-30, handing the jubilant Welsh a memorable victory.

But despite their disappointment England took solace that they were undoubtedly an improving side. Impressed by the intimidating cauldron in Cardiff, Lancaster set about an ambitious project to make Twickenham Stadium England's extra man.

A new ritual was introduced in 2014, whereby the players would approach the West concourse on foot 90 minutes before kick-off to allow the English supporters to show their appreciation for their team. It paid immediate dividends. Superhuman defensive efforts from new second-row combination Joe Launchbury and Courtney Lawes, allied to the uncompromising attacking intent of full-back Mike Brown, imbued new character in the developing side. Hugely impressive home victories against both Ireland and Wales helped England to their first Triple Crown since the record-breaking 2003 season. It, along with the defeat of the All Blacks in 2012, will be seen as important markers as England build towards the all-important 2015 season.

Jonny Wilkinson, England
v. Italy, 2011.

England *v.* Ireland, 2014.

Twickenham Stadium, 2011.

Above: The Triple Crown on display in World Rugby Museum, 2014.

Above left: Toby Flood, 2011.

Left: England *v.* Wales, 2011.

Right: England *v.* Barbarians, 2012.

Above: England fans, 2009.

Left: England fans.

Right: Owen Farrell, England *v.* Wales, 2014.

35

England 2015

The RFU had received only three votes when bidding for the 2007 Rugby World Cup, two of which were their own. The tournament was awarded to France and the RFU went back to the drawing board.

In the long-run, however, the French tournament did have a positive impact in the RFU's efforts to return the tournament to Twickenham. RWC 2007 made a profit, the following tournament in New Zealand in 2011 did not. It was therefore decided that the future bidding process would select the following two host nations, one of which would be from an established rugby playing nation, the other from a developing rugby playing nation.

In 2009, it was announced that England had beaten off competition from Italy and South Africa, and would host the eighth edition of the Rugby World Cup, to be held in 2015. The trophy, named after William Webb Ellis, would be returning to his place of birth.

Included in the RFU's bid proposal were projections for the sale of over 2 million tickets, as well as a commercial return of £220 million from broadcasting, sponsorship and merchandise. If the pledge was fulfilled, the tournament would be the largest and most profitable rugby tournament of all time by some considerable distance.

Twickenham Stadium would be all-important in the attainment of such exacting criteria.

Group of Death

The preliminary draw was made in 2012 and immediately threw up talking points, not least that had England had been selected in Pool A, alongside Australia and Wales. So that England 2015 might sell their full allocation of tickets, Cardiff's Millennium Stadium was expected to host a number of fixtures. Roger Lewis, of the Welsh Rugby Union, even suggested that the England *v*. Wales pool fixture should be held there. RFU chief executive Ian Ritchie's reply returned the humour of the request, 'we have a … modest little stadium here at Twickenham, with a little further investment we might be able to make it into a decent spot to play rugby,' he replied.

The following year, it became clear that Twickenham Stadium was to be the bedrock upon which the tournament would be built. All but one of England's pool games would be held there. To ensure neutrality beyond the home nation, the crucial Wales *v.* Australia pool match would also be held there, along with two quarter-finals, both semi-finals and the final itself.

The England Dressing Room

Before that would come a series of innovative alterations to the stadium's internal fabric. The England dressing room had been through a number of changes since the West Stand had opened in 1995. Clive Woodward, in the interests of giving his players a bit more privacy, had altered the position of the door into the player's tunnel. He had also requested that a series of golden plaques listing and detailed many of England's greatest victories were put up on the walls of the tunnel for the benefit of England's opponents.

The plaques lasted until 2007 when Brian Ashton settled on a simpler method of communicating the spirit of the place. Having taken the plaques away, he had the walls painted white with a large red cross on either facing wall.

Stuart Lancaster, however, decided that the side's past was to be a marker for the future. Murals depicting the many triumphs of the English side were brought into the corridor that linked the tunnel with the outer concourse. The entrance to the dressing room was moved once again, with a new corridor now linking them to the player's tunnel. The interior of this area was devoted solely to the psychology of those privileged enough to enter. Etched into the walls are England's greatest achievements. A roll of honour listing every man to have represented England since 1871 is on one wall of the dressing room. Behind each player's jersey are listed ten former players, arranged according to position, underneath the words 'One of Us'. Above is a plaque, bearing each player's name and the England rose. These

have long been assigned to players, but Lancaster made one simple alteration. Now every player is issued a number that determines their place in a sequence, dating all the way back to 1871.

It is fitting that the stadium, which last hosted the tournament when only the North Stand of its completed form was present, should now host it when it is complete. There is no question that 2015 will be the greatest Rugby World Cup there has ever been and that Twickenham Stadium, its heritage and sporting legacy, will be its most iconic monument.

England fans. 2013.

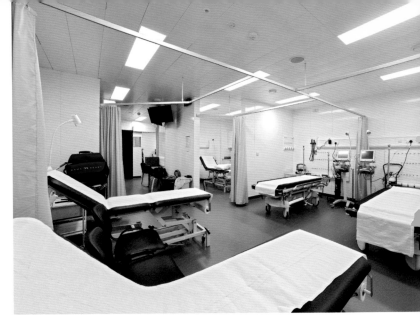

Above: Medical centre, 2013.

Above and below left: England dressing room, 2013.

Right: Ian Ritchie, 2012.

Above: Players' tunnel, 2013.

Above left: Pitch flags.

Left: North car park by night, 2010.

Right: Ten-year anniversary dinner, 2013., showing the Webb Ellis Cup